FIGHTING FOR YOUR LIFE

Man-eater Bears

To Roha Parcy -
Remember - you don't have
to outrun the bear, just
your friend.

Tom Hron

3/08/14

For information about this title or to order other books and/or electronic
media, contact the publisher:

Proman, Incorporated
P.O. Box 19960, Fountain Hills, Arizona 85269-9960
info@packalarm.net
480-837-5855

ISBN: 978-0-9840515-9-5

Printed in the United States of America

Book and Cover design by: 1106 Design

ACKNOWLEDGMENTS AND DEDICATION

W HERE DO YOU BEGIN when you have spent so much of your life flying the Far North and meeting all the legendary characters who pioneered the place—Don Braun, the first man to land a wheeled airplane at the North Pole; Ray Petersen, an early 1900s bush pilot and "Father of Alaska's Sports Fishing Lodges," as recognized by its state legislature in 1999; Don and Warren Johnson, incomparable pilots and master guides from the time of Alaskan statehood; and all the wonderful men and women who have won similar fame in the vast wilderness that stretches from Hudson Bay to the Bering Sea. I have been lucky beyond belief to meet so many extraordinary people, and I dedicate this book to all of them.

I would like to specially thank Pat Dougherty, Editor of the *Anchorage Daily News,* and Rod Boyce, Managing Editor of the *Fairbanks Daily News-Miner,* since both represent the two great newspapers of Alaska that I've read for so long. It was always fascinating to get those out-of-breath phone calls saying, "Hey, did you hear that so-and-so just crashed his airplane?" or "My God, have you heard so-and-so just got killed by a bear?" and then the next day read about it in my sales office on Lake Hood, the world's largest floatplane base at the Anchorage International Airport. For twenty years, I sat in what I often called the "catbird seat" and listened to the most incredible stories one could ever imagine, which more often than not turned out to be woefully true. Derek Neary of the Northern News Services in Yellowknife, Northwest Territories, Canada, is another person I'd like to thank for helping me with this book. His instant friendship is what I've always loved about the North.

The Alaska Department of Public Safety (State and Wildlife Troopers) were a great assistance as well, since their case files were invaluable as I completed my research. Ted Spraker, retired wildlife biologist and Alaska Board of Game vice chair, was another source of important information. He knows his bears, to say the least. I want to thank Gary Youngblood of the Gates of the Arctic National Park for his help as well.

Last but not least, I want to thank Ron Davis of Soldotna and "Red" and Judy Wagner of Anchorage for their enduring support. All three have always taken the time to help me in any way they could, and their kindness has meant a lot to me through the years. Loyal friends are true friends indeed.

PLAY DEAD

I T WAS 1:45 ON A GRAY AFTERNOON on October 5, 2003. The Katmai Coast had rolled under a gale all day and Kaflia Lake's whitecaps were prickling with wind-driven rain. Timothy Treadwell and Amie Huguenard were waiting inside their tent for better weather—Andrew Airways wouldn't fly out of Kodiak until the Shelikof Strait's visibility improved and the winds let down. Willy Fulton, their bush pilot, was a good friend but he wasn't any fool, not in the kind of weather that had killed so many Alaskans just like him.

Tim heard it first and since he was always antsy anyway, he crawled outside for a look. Amie zipped up the tent's fly to keep out the wind and rain.

The tent was flagging like torn sailcloth, but she still could hear him walking around. Then she heard something else as well. *"Huff—phh. Huff—phh. Arrrrrrrrr..."* Had a bear woofed and snarled under its breath? she wondered.

Next, she heard Tim shout, "Stop. Go away. Stop it!"

Suddenly, there was a muffled impact and something hit the ground.

"Huff-phh. Arrrrrrrrrr!" It was much louder this time.

She switched on their camcorder, but left the cover on the lens. It was 1:47.

"Help me," screamed Tim, "I'm getting killed!"

Amie unzipped the tent's fly, which added another snarl of sorts to all the background noise.

"Play dead—play dead," she shouted back. After that, she left the tent and started screaming in sheer terror.

Treadwell did what he was told and the bear backed off, no doubt surprised by Amie's unexpected appearance, but then Mr. Vicious must have decided to finish the job once and for all, since Amie was obviously no threat. The attack began again, except it was a lot bloodier this time.

"Hit it," shrieked Tim. "Hit it with the pan."

"Fight back," answered Amie. Moments afterward, there was a noise almost like a muted bell. "Get away, get away. Let go, let go. Go away, go away," she screamed time after time. *Was she actually beating on the bear with a frying pan?*

Tim's cries then faded as he was being dragged into the alders to be eaten alive.

Amie screams went out of control, turned eerily rhythmic, and then the tape stopped. It was 1:53.

Then after another *"Arrrrrrrrr"* and something sounding like a big pillow fight, she finally stopped screaming. The gale rolled on, but now there was the sound of her body being torn apart in front of the tent.

 # BLOODY MURDER

I CAN'T GET THEIR SCREAMS OUT OF MY HEAD—Kathy Huffman Jacqueline Perry, Marcie Trent, Darcy Staver, Adelia Maestas Trujillo, and Amie Huguenard's, of course. I could go on and on—all the women who have been killed by bears—except what good would it do me? Then there was five-month-old Ester Schwimmer and six-year-old Elora Petrasek. What makes it even worse is some of them were eaten like so much sausage. Guess I'm old-fashioned since I think women and children are special, so maybe that's why their shrieks won't go away, even though I never really heard them. I keep thinking everything could have been prevented and their ghosts wouldn't haunt me.

There have been plenty of men killed and eaten too, with Tim Dexter, a.k.a. Timothy Treadwell of *Grizzly Man* fame, being by far the best known, but for some odd reason that doesn't bother me as much. Maybe it's because most bear experts favor the double entendre *"leading role"* or the label *"poster boy"* when they talk about him. Or maybe because the TV documentary about him was so fascinating on the one hand and so disturbing on the other I'm left with nothing more than the horrific way

Amie had to go, let alone all the others. —she had begged to leave Upper Kaflia Lake, but he wouldn't listen to her. *By God, he wasn't going to listen to anyone when it came to bears,* which has sent us backward to the trigger-happy days of the 1900s. It took just six and a half minutes of camcorder audio to flush everything down the toilet—his work as an ecowarrior, the amazing photography, the NBC *Dateline* and The Discovery Channel specials, his guest appearances on "David Letterman," and all the exciting presentations he'd given to schoolchildren, which may turn out to be the biggest disaster of all. *What in hell do we tell them now?*

The attacks on Tim and Amie were solely predatory and proven beyond any doubt by the removal of their body parts from Mr. Vicious, the nickname Tim had given the bear that killed them. The trouble is no one will ever know what *actually* happened—the soundtrack didn't start until after Tim had been knocked down, and then it stopped sometime prior to Amie being killed. How long she lived, nobody knows. To make matters worse, there was so much background noise—wind, rain, screaming—and to further complicate things, so many nuanced statements by state and federal authorities later on, some of whom I know, it's arguable about what was being said anyway. Or maybe I should say screamed and cursed in this case, since Treadwell had a propensity for using the F-bomb when he was stressed. Last but not least, an ex-girlfriend of his seized the audiotape and threatened everyone with all kinds of lawsuits, then supposedly destroyed it. I somehow doubt this, but it really doesn't matter. My dramatized account of the attack is close enough for government work, which is where it all ended up anyway, for what little good it did anybody. *People are still playing with bears!*...although now I'm getting ahead of myself.

Amie's death has always angered me—she was so ill prepared for the situation she found herself in it's been difficult for
me to grasp the enormity of it. City girl, no wilderness skills,
and nearly clueless when it came to bear safety and how to
survive an attack by one. Then to make matters worse, she was
hooked up with a certifiable loony who'd been told a million
times, "You're gonna get yourself killed if you keep messing
with those bears." Unfortunately, none of it seemed to matter
since she still let him browbeat her into something she didn't
want to do, which then got her killed in the most hideous way
possible. What's even more upsetting, she didn't need to die
at all, not if she'd known what to do. I'll write more about Tim
and Amie later, since their deaths are almost as classic as it gets
when it comes to making fatal mistakes around bears.

Michio Hoshino was another bear enthusiast who was killed
and eaten, although he wasn't a loony tune like Treadwell. This
man was almost legendary in Alaska for his wildlife photography,
with the likes of *National Geographic* featuring his work. What's
more, he'd successfully published three popular titles, *Grizzly*,
The Grizzly Bear Family Book, and *Moose*, which, along with his
other publications, had made him a virtual rock star in Japan,
his homeland. He had even won that country's highest honor
for photographers in 1990. We had crossed paths and I knew
a little about him, since my wife had studied black-and-white
nature photography under a contemporary of his, Sam Kimura,
a professor emeritus at the University of Alaska. Michio was no
flake, but he was flawed, much as I hate to say.

In 1996, he'd flown to Kurilskoya Lake on the Kamchatka
Peninsula to take pictures of its brown bears, which are the
counterpart of Alaska's biggest ones. They generally run a
bit smaller, but otherwise are just as dangerous. Why Michio
would fly to Russia for something he could easily find at home is

something of a mystery to me, other than I suppose he'd worked there a few times before and Kamchatka isn't all that far from Japan, where his photos had always sold like hotcakes. In any case, off he went to the remote Kurilskoya wildlife refuge with his passport and the required permit in hand.

He was also legendary for sleeping outdoors, sometimes in his tent, other times with nothing more than a sleeping bag and a foam-rubber mattress. The guy was an animal when it came to waiting for just the right picture, once having lived on the Tokositna Glacier for a month in the dead of winter to get a shot of the northern lights over Denali, the highest mountain in North America. I came of age in Northern Minnesota and then lived for twenty years in Alaska, and so there's very little I don't know about the cold, but you couldn't get me to do that at the point of a gun. I'd much rather die right on the spot and get it over with quickly, and Michio's middle name was "Frostbite" because he was so tough. Live in a meat locker if you want to know what it's like.

When he reached Kurilskoya Lake, he was told a bear had just broken into the lone cabin that served the refuge, however, the supervising biologists said they had fixed the damage and there was room for him inside. He refused and told them he'd rather sleep outside. "Nyet, nyet," the Russians warned. "The bear keeps coming back and pepper spray doesn't even work." The charismatic Michio just laughed, since he'd once camped at Brooks Falls in the Katmai National Park (where brown bears are always catching salmon in midair) and heard something snoring up against his tent's sidewall. A big bear had decided to catch a few winks right alongside him.

The hooligan bear continued its assaults on the cabin and its adjacent food cache, coming in at night and trying its best to tear into one or the other building. It even went to the extent of climbing on top of the food shed and jumping up and down on its tin roof, which made so much racket that it led to one of the refuge biologists shooting at it with pepper spray from fifteen feet. The cone-shaped mist fell short, the bear sniffed at it, and then went on with its business. Everyone in camp banged pots and pans, screamed at the top of their lungs, and shot more pepper spray, but nothing worked. The bear simply ducked to one side or the other and seemed to enjoy the smell of the repellent (I'll talk more about this phenomenon in a later chapter). Despite the bear coming right up to his tent, Michio wouldn't budge. He had once written in one of his books, "People continue to tame and subjugate nature, but when we visit the few remaining scraps of wilderness where bears roam free, we can still feel an instinctive fear. How precious that feeling is." That all sounds quite wonderful, though I find it a bit sanctimonious since it cheapens human life, but what's important is Michio had forgotten the value of his own.

He had come to the United States on a tramp ship, knocked around Los Angeles and New York a little, then moved to Shishmaref, an Inupiat village on the Bering Straits. Talk about stark contrast, this one would be hard to beat. Nonetheless, he settled in with a Native-Alaskan family and learned to love the Arctic with a passion. Later, he went back home and studied under Japan's best nature photographer, then in 1978 moved to Alaska for good. Friends would find him in the most inhospitable places imaginable waiting for just the right shot. It made little difference that he knew almost nothing about animals, couldn't afford anything but junk cars, and only spoke broken English. For example, one of his favorite sayings was, "Oh, you poolin' my fool." Everyone loved him, and no one had more charm, desire, or artistic talents all rolled up into one.

The one thing missing was a family all his own. Whenever he visited friends, he'd start rolling around the floor with their kids, playing with them until they were carted off to bed. But with his lifestyle, it was hard to meet someone who'd want to be his wife. Finally, after seeing the movie, *Moonstruck,* he got serious about it and told friends he wanted to be moonstruck as well. Afterward, he met Naoko and they had a son named Shoma. —this is what I meant when I said he'd forgotten the worth of his own life. At some point you must tell yourself, "My life isn't mine anymore, and I can't do this because my family will always need me."

The bear ripped into Michio's tent and dragged him out in the pitch black of a predawn morning. His wailing cries woke all the people in the cabin, but it was too late by the time they got out there. Using flashlights, they found the bear eating him back in the weeds, but it only glanced up when they tried chasing it away by banging on a water pail with a shovel. Pepper spray, noise, nothing worked, and they had no guns because they were prohibited at Kurilskoya. Finally, the bear grabbed Michio's rag-doll remains in its teeth, ran into the woods, and that was the last of him, but for his bones.

Everyone abandoned the cabin and used a boat and motor to look for help from across the lake, and later on several well-armed men returned and searched for the bear and Michio's body, although without any luck. The woods were simply too thick and there weren't enough of them for a thorough search, even though it was now broad daylight. Finally, a helicopter showed up with a professional hunter on board and not long afterward the pilot flushed the bear out of its hideout. There was an ensuing gun barrage along Kurilskoya's lakeshore and the bear was knocked down, but as often happens with bears, it got back up and escaped again the moment the helicopter landed. Off the pilot went once more, and after another wild chase and hail of bullets, it fell for good.

Lest you think that people are only killed and eaten in Alaska and Russia, let's give New York State a try, which, for all practical purposes, is an entirely different world. Amazingly, it took just the blink of an eye for Ester Schwimmer of Brooklyn to lose her life, the five-month-old baby I mentioned in my first paragraph. Even George Pataki, the governor, was brokenhearted by this attack, since it involved a friend of his, and the Big Apple's anti-hunting attitude would take an instant hit. Understandably, bears don't look so great when they start grabbing babies right from under their mother's noses.

Ester was sleeping in her stroller on a bungalow porch in Fallsburg, which isn't much north of New Jersey. Lots of families holiday there for its pastoral settings and fine recreational opportunities such as camping, fishing, and hiking. Black bears love the area as well and their numbers have been increasing exponentially because of it. Lots of woods to hide in and food sources galore, such as garbage cans, dog food, and bird feeders, so what more could they ask for, especially since no one has taken a shot at them since 1970, when bear hunting was banned. There had been 1,350 complaints, including 58 home invasions in New Jersey alone, let alone in New York State itself, around the time Ester was killed, so it wasn't like folks were unaware of the danger. Still, Fallsburg wasn't the sort of place you'd expect one to run off with your baby.

At around 2 p.m. Ester's mom heard someone yell, "Bear, bear, there's a bear right here." She pushed her two other small kids inside and then rushed to get her baby girl as well, but it was already too late by the time she got back to the porch. The bear had grabbed Ester by the head and took off for the woods, which was only a few jumps away. People chased after it and threw as many rocks as they could, and that got Ester dropped to the ground, but the bites were too deep for her to survive.

She was pronounced dead at the hospital a little while later, shocking everyone along the East Coast.

Adelia Maestas Trujillo is another death that would make most folks' hair stand on end, leastwise if they live where there's a large population of black bears as around Fallsburg. She was a teensy 93-year-old great-grandmother who lived by herself near Cleveland, New Mexico, a town of 600 or so residents in the north-central part of the state. One night she woke to an odd noise and went to investigate, only to see a black bear smash through the screen window in her kitchen door and come after her. Needless to say, there wasn't much of a struggle, but what her son found the next day must have been more than anyone is meant to endure.

The various law enforcement officials such as the county sheriff, a state medical examiner, and two wildlife officers all described the attack in the usual doublespeak, which in my mind was secret code for saying the poor woman was chewed to the bone. In addition, they hastily explained how unusual the predation was and speculated the bear might have been hurt or Adelia had somehow scared it into killing her, which was not only farfetched but sounded awfully silly since she was only the size of a schoolgirl. Last of all, they opined all the berries and acorns had been destroyed by spring frosts and a summer drought, so the bears were hungry (for crying out loud, they're always hungry). Whatever the reasons for her death, some trackers with dogs soon found a bear in the general vicinity and shot it, and then it was taken away for a necropsy, the surgical procedure that looks for human remains, rabies, and crippling injuries.

By now you should see something of a pattern in the attacks I've described and how everyone dealt with all the bloody carnage from beginning to end, whether it was the victim or the person or persons who came along afterward, which, I might add, is the quintessence of this book. *We learn from other people's mistakes!* Always have, always will...*except*, it seems, when it comes to bears, which has left a good many folks dead, if not disfigured for life. For some reason we don't seem to *"get it"* when it comes to dealing with them, yet we insist they be preserved and multiplied if at all possible. That's a recipe for ever-increasing calamities, since we have two burgeoning populations trying to occupy the same space. Something's got to give, and so there's no misunderstanding I don't necessarily think it should be the bears. People need to smarten up.

"Well, what in hell do you know?" you might ask. —fair question, but rather than bore you with my background, I'll tell you a true story and let you decide for yourself what I might know.

My birthday is on the sixth of July, and my wife, Sharon, and I usually kill two birds with one stone and stretch Independence Day into a double-barreled celebration. Since we often go somewhere, on one Fourth of July we decided to fly to Bear Lake, which is about a hundred miles north of where the Alaskan Peninsula turns into the Aleutian Islands at an abandoned World War II airbase called Cold Bay. This is where the Bering Sea meets the North Pacific and creates some of the worst weather in the world. If you like warp-speed winds and horizontal rain and snow, this is the place for you, although I'd suggest you live in a bomb shelter rather than a trailer house. And there's a few of them around, bomb shelters that is, since this is one of the places where the Japanese made war on us in 1942. It's almost impossible to describe this land in terms of its magnificence, rich history, snowcapped mountains, live volcanoes, brutal weather, and, most important of all, profusion of wildlife, with the biggest brown bears in the world topping the food chain. I once saw one that weighed nearly a ton, and I'm not kidding. Now when this one crapped in the woods, you really knew about it (sorry for my shot at some humor, but I don't want to be accused of only being ghoulish when I write).

We left Anchorage in our Cessna 185, which is a high-wing, single-engine, tail-wheeled airplane that can be compared to driving a Chevy Corvette. It's six-place, fast, and can be used on floats, wheels, or skis, and is arguably the best bush plane that's ever been built. I should also add that Alaska has very few roads and if you want to go someplace you are usually down to two choices—an airplane or a boat. Life's not so great if you get airsick or seasick all the time.

I've flown airplanes and helicopters all over North America since 1962, so there's little I haven't seen involving busy airports, but I have to admit there's nothing quite like flying in and out of the Anchorage International Airport. It's what anyone would expect of any major airport that serves numerous international carriers such as China, Japan, and Northwest Airlines, but right in the middle of everything is a gravel landing strip and a seaplane base with 1,500 little airplanes coming and going all day long. Flying around Anchorage is a lot more like dog fighting over Berlin in World War II with a bomber wing thrown into the middle of everything than in the tranquility one might see, for example, at Sky Harbor in Phoenix, Arizona. Kamikaze alley is what I call it, because it's the world's third busiest cargo airport as well. Go kick a beehive if you want to know what it's like.

To make things even *more* interesting, your arrivals and departures are either over Knik Arm or Turnagain Arm, two riptide channels that come off Cook Inlet, which is infamous for its thirty-foot tides. You can't help but look down at that boiling brown water and wonder what would happen if your engine ever quit, which happens from time to time. Sad to say you haven't a prayer, but at least the last thing you will see is the most beautiful mountain in North America, Mount McKinley, or what Alaskans call Denali, way off in the distance. Hopefully, it would work out to be some kind of religious experience for you. I had used the Lake Hood Airstrip for my takeoff, which is the formal name of the gravel strip I'd mentioned on the international airport, then climbed out over Knik Arm and what's called the Duck Flats, the northern tidelands of Cook Inlet. One of the reasons for our trip was to look for bears, and the month of July is the perfect time for it. Most are feeding on the salmon that are running up the rivers, so it's easy to find them. Bear viewing has grown into a big-time business in Alaska with millions of dollars involved, but as usual it's getting way overdone, which I'll vent my angst about later on. Anyway, it wasn't long before my wife and I started seeing bears by the dozens...but little did we know that we'd soon get more than we had bargained for.

It's sad that most people never get to see the real Alaska in all its glory. The state is so vast, rugged, and remote it's almost impossible for most folks to do much more than hit the hotspots. The only alternative is to own a bush plane and have the time, money, and proficiency to use it, but even then everything's a major expedition where you must be prepared to live for Lord knows how long under survival conditions. One day the weather is paradise and you fly from Anchorage through, let's say, Merrill Pass to the Stony River on the other side of the Alaskan Mountain Range. This trip is so breathtaking I've seen veteran adventurers who've bragged they've seen it all suddenly fall silent and get tears in their eyes. The problem is once you get there and camp overnight you often find yourself stuck in a cold, miserable rain that won't quit. Everything gets so sopping wet you can't keep a fire going with a barrel of jet fuel. *Now what?* You better have the patience and survival skills to wait it out, or else.

The reason I bring this up is it's almost impossible to go *anyplace* in Alaska without flying through one of its mountain passes, and Merrill in particular is extremely nasty even when the weather is nice. When the weather's bad...well, it's suicidal to try flying through there. To prove my point, there's sixty-some airplane wrecks scattered along its mountainsides, turning it into the state's greatest bone yard in more ways than one. The ghosts of a good many people live there, and Merrill is best left to its ethereal solitude as far as I'm concerned. Sadly, some of those poor souls were people I knew.

We flew Cook Inlet's coastline all the way down to Kamishak Bay, which took us past the best brown bear country in the world. It doesn't take long and you literally lose count of them, since you're flying over every hotspot there is, such as Polly Creek, the Crescent River, Chinitna Bay, Bruin Bay (aptly named), and, most important of all, the McNeil River Game Sanctuary, where folks wait on a lottery for years to visit. There's no other place on earth where it's commonplace to see sixty bears gathered at a single river falls, and since the state runs it with an iron fist and only lets in ten people a day, you must wait in line, or better said, stay online and hope you hit the jackpot. Understandably, you're competing with people from all over for the Holy Grail of bear viewing.

The scenery on the way to McNeil River would make the flight worthwhile even if there weren't any bears at all, since you have the Alaskan Mountain Range off your right and the Augustine Volcano on your left out in an ocean bay. I stayed low and slow and we soaked it all in—the bears, the volcanoes, and the fjords running back into the sea cliffs. It's almost impossible to describe Alaska's magnificence in simple words, since one has to see it to believe it. The colors spellbind you.

Start with a sky so blue you can see distant peaks hundreds of miles away, then add the gleaming white of countless snow-caps reflecting yellow sunlight back into the air. Come down a little and the colors turn to gray mountains towering over green valleys. Next it becomes blue once again on the brown bottomlands where the ocean meets the beaches, bounded by foaming whitecaps as the surf rolls in. Finally, add the black volcanoes belching their steam into the wind and make believe you're right in the middle of everything. I hope I've mesmerized you with the breathtaking beauty of this panorama, as it doesn't come any better, and, frankly, it was the nicest birthday present ever given to me.

We set a new course at McNeil for King Salmon, a fishing settlement not far from Bristol Bay, the greatest fish factory under the sun. Try almost forty million sockeye salmon alone gathering in its waters for their annual migration up the rivers ending there, then add the countless millions of the other salmon species as well. That's a hundred million fish every summer, and it's no wonder the Aleuts, Eskimos, and Indians weren't so thrilled when the Russians crashed their party in the early 1800s. Other than for the bears and the bloodsucking bugs, there was little for them to complain about, since this was as good as it got in primitive times. They certainly didn't face any food shortages, not with all the caribou and moose that abounded as well.

It's simply amazing the number of bears that congregate in the country between McNeil and King Salmon, which is the northern half of the Katmai National Park. We flew over the Kulik River and Brooks Falls shaking our heads in wonder, since it's hard to believe there are places where bears still outnumber the people, although it's getting pretty close at Brooks. Seaplanes haul tourists in and out by the dozens every day, leaving the place looking a lot more like an airport than unique parkland. There are two bearing-viewing platforms along the Brooks River, with the one at the falls that holds forty people. Understandably, it's a busy place.

We landed at the King Salmon Airport, gassed up, and took off south along the coastline of Bristol Bay, which, presuming your geography is bad, is part of the Bering Sea. There are a few fishing villages along the way, Naknek, Egegik, Pilot Point, and Port Heiden, but for the most part there's nothing but the wind, the seawater, and an endless black sand beach all the way to Cold Bay, which, once again, isn't the end of the world...but you can see it from there (my second shot at a little humor). I can't emphasize enough how isolated the Alaskan Peninsula is along its entire length with things you would never see anywhere else, like brown bears hunting walrus. Eskimos and polar bears aren't the only ones who have developed a taste for them, and there's a special place where the browns have gotten into the act too. *Pssssst, most bear experts don't even know about this, let alone the scientists who study walrus.*

The landscape south of King Salmon is undulating wetlands with a jillion lakes, which are home for the same number of waterbirds. White swans, sandhill cranes, and every duck imaginable spend their summers here, bounded by the Bering Sea on the west and snowcapped volcanoes on the east, the North Pacific side of the Alaskan Peninsula. It's not very far across, especially with an airplane, and gets narrower as you travel south. It's a nice place to fly, presuming the weather's good, because you can land almost anywhere on the unending beach. Your greatest hazard would be hitting one of the countless eagles, seagulls, red fox, and brown bear that are flocking to the many salmon streams that run into the sea.

Bear Lake is the best place on the whole peninsula, besides being about the only place where you can stay. It consists of a rustic lodge and a separate, motel-like structure that sits out the back door, with both overlooking the lake and a fine-looking river by the same name. It's all self-contained with the requisite outbuildings, landing strip, generators, dining room, and bar-room with a spectacular view of the snowcapped mountains off to the east.

The lodge site was discovered somewhat by accident by a big-game guide named Don Johnson in the mid-1950s when he was flying someone around who was searching for White Alice locations, which were the tropospheric scatter and microwave radio link facilities that served the Distant Early Warning or DEW-line radar sites in the Cold War with Russia. This was all very top-secret back then and, of course, was this nation's first-warning system against the Soviet Union attacking us with their nuclear bombers. Don ran into some shitty weather with his two-seat Piper Super Cub and had to plunk it down before he got trapped by fog. *Walla!* he found Bear Lake, aptly named for the countless browns that wander the place. It's another one of those Alaskan wonders that's hard to describe in simple words.

To show you how special Bear Lake is, when Prince Bandar of Saudi Arabia, the ambassador to the United States until 2005, wanted to go bear hunting guess who he called...well, at least Don's son, Warren, who now runs Bear Lake, as Don has passed away. The prince rented the entire lodge lock, stock, and gun barrel, if you catch what I mean, then showed up with an entourage fit for a king, which he is more or less. Warren said that he's never in his life seen such an air force of airplanes and helicopters, all parked alongside his garden-sized landing strip. Almost every VIP in the world who wants to go bear hunting calls him because his lodge is so amazingly located, and he's seldom had to advertise since it's so well-known by the grand safari crowd. I've had the good fortune of having Warren as a friend for many years, and there's no one in the world who's more charismatic or a better bush pilot. I could write a whole book alone about his adventures, and he's proven time and again that he has more lives than the proverbial cat.

We landed with the required pucker factor on Warren's bush runway, tied down our Cessna with his ship-anchor ropes, since the wind blows with such velocity, and said hello to his wife, Marlie. He was off commercial fishing and would be back the next day. We were soon settled in a corner bedroom on the bottom floor where all the guests stay, which happened to be right under where Marlie was sleeping.

Sharon and I spent the afternoon and evening in a reverse fishing contest, which is a game where you try retrieving your lure *without* catching anything. In July, the sockeye salmon gather at the head of the Bear River in such great numbers the water turns black with them, and it becomes quite a contest to cast out and not catch one as you crank back your bait. Meanwhile, we would see bears in the distance itching to come down to a nearby fish weir where an Alaska state employee in a rundown cabin was counting the summer spawn. When he'd quit for the day, the bears would sneak in and steal fish from behind the holding gate, which turned out to be a perfect place for my wife to take some beautiful pictures of a monster brown. Bear Lake is magical, and people have thought so for thousands of years. The lakeshore is covered with ancient Aleut mizzens dating back thousands of years, and it's clear hundreds of people lived there at one time.

That night we played cards with Marlie and her staff, then hit the sack. We were both dog-tired from the long flight and the time we'd spent fishing. Sharon took the bed by the outside corner of the building and I climbed into one near a window about head-high above the floor, though it was covered with a thick blue curtain to keep out the midnight sun. We fell asleep in moments.

Crack!

It sounded like a two-by-four wall stud had snapped and woke me. I couldn't figure out what was going on and in the dark decided my wife had slapped the bedroom wall for some odd reason.

"For crying out loud, will you stop that, because I'm trying to sleep."

A little voice answered from the other side of the room. "I didn't do anything."

I laid there for a moment and thought things over. "What in hell?" I wondered.

I jumped out of bed, jerked the curtain to one side, and, since it was a bit dark out, pressed my nose against the window and stared out. At first, I didn't see anything.

Suddenly, a stovepipe-sized nose with two beady eyes rose up and filled the window. I've never been so shocked in my life, since I was now nose-to-nose with a huge brown.

I started pounding on the wall and yelling, "Get back, get back, get out of here." The racket was less than two feet from the bear's ears.

In what seemed like an eternity, the bear finally dropped back onto all fours and wandered away, not looking the least bit frightened or surprised. I watched as it walked toward the lake, then climbed back into my bed. Needless to say, I lay awake for a while.

The next morning I woke up before Sharon, dressed, and walked around to the outside corner of the building. I had a good idea what had made the loud crack.

The brown had walked up to the corner, bit into it, and split off a baseball-bat-sized chunk of trim. The wood looked like someone had taken a pickax after it.

I walked across to the dining room, shaking my head in amazement. The bear had chomped into the building within a foot of Sharon's head. Why she hadn't come flying out of bed, I'll never know, since the whole episode had scared the daylights out of me.

When I walked into the dining room for my breakfast, Marlie instantly started acting funny. She looked embarrassed and obviously didn't want to talk to me. Suddenly, it dawned on me. She thought my wife and I had gotten into a big fight in the middle of the night and made a terrible scene.

"Didn't you hear all that noise last night?" I asked.

"No-no." She wouldn't look up.

"A bear was trying to break into our bedroom."

Her eyes shot straight at me. "What?"

"A big brown walked up to where we were sleeping and ripped a big chunk out of the building. You won't believe the piece it took out."

"Oh, my God, that's what that was." She headed for the door.

We walked across and examined the damage. Marlie had never liked living around bears and she wasn't at all amused.

"I've told Warren a thousand times to fix that south door. That bear could have pushed right in and come upstairs."

Now it was my turn to be surprised. "The door just down the hallway from us?"

"Yes, it never closes. It's warped and won't lock."

Holy cow—there had to be a way to fix that door!

I've had numerous run-ins like this with bears and have learned a lot from them. Let me share my experiences in the coming chapters.

# THE BLACK PLAGUE

ALL BEARS WILL KILL AND EAT YOU if given the right opportunity, and your safety depends on your familiarity with the behavior of the different species. Regrettably, the existing information on bears is wrong or very misleading and endangers everyone when he or she goes on an outdoor adventure.

There are three kinds of bears in North America, the black, the grizzly, and the polar, but we will make believe there are four in this book. The grizzly comes in two varieties—the common species that's found in Montana, Idaho, Canada, and Alaska's interior, and the subspecies that's called the brown bear and/or the Kodiak, which is found along Alaska's seacoasts. Size is the only difference between the two. A big grizzly might weigh six or seven hundred pounds, but a brown will commonly weigh twice as much, or as I often like to say, *"they're not a lot smaller than Volkswagens."* Browns have gotten oversized because of their gene pool and rich diet of salmon.

The black bear lives almost everywhere in North America and is the hardest to profile. I've run into them in Alaska where they've never seen humans before, and I've run into them in national parks where they see humans almost every day. There is great danger in both places, particularly if you follow the advice of the so-called experts. Believing that bears are more scared than you are (who's ever interviewed one, anyway), banging pots and pans, waving your arms, and lying down as if you are dead is a good way to get yourself mauled, if not killed and eaten. Let me tell two true stories to make my point.

My wife and I flew our Robinson R22 helicopter into a gold claim that we own along a white-water river one hundred miles north of Anchorage. The R22 sounds like flying farm machinery and even frightens people, let alone wildlife. I started clearing an ATV trail with a chainsaw and Sharon climbed a steep hill and worked on a spring we wanted to use for drinking water. It was a perfect day in a true wilderness setting, and all was wonderful.

I shut off the saw and piled the trees and brush that I had cut, then stood for a moment catching my breath. Something rustled in the distance but I didn't think much of it, and so I restarted the saw and went back to work. Sharon walked up behind me a little while later and I stopped again. We spoke and then I heard another noise, so I looked off in that direction.

I couldn't believe my eyes because a black bear was stalking us and had snuck within two hundred feet without me noticing. The bear froze when I pointed at it and exclaimed, "Look at that," showing my wife where it stood. Although it was adult-sized, I wasn't afraid because I had the saw, but I was puzzled over its odd behavior. I started the saw once more, revved it up, and marched toward the bear like the Texas chainsaw murderer, certain it would run away. All I got was a nasty surprise.

The bear postured with its back arched, hair on end, and popped its teeth, its way of letting me know it was unwilling to back off, let alone run away. —so much for bears being more frightened than you are, which has always been complete nonsense. That has more to do with hunting pressure than anything else. Bears that are regularly hunted wise up in a hurry and seldom want anything to do with people, the reverse of those found in the national parks where they are often fed. I routinely check the hunting seasons of a given area to help me assess the risk of encountering a predatory bear.

I turned away, kept the saw running, and my wife and I walked back to our helicopter where I had left my .44 magnum revolver. We hoped the bear would move off and leave us alone, and so we spent some time standing around. Twenty minutes later we returned to my worksite with the .44 and, wouldn't you know, the bear was waiting for us. I was sure one shot would scare the daylights out of it, so I marched forward again and let drive with a shot over its head. The bear hardly flinched. *What in hell is going on?* I wondered, but I kept on marching and fired once more. This time the bear turned sideways and shuffled off a few steps. I blasted away a third time and finally the bear broke into a half-hearted retreat. I chased after it with my fiercest war cry and fired a fourth time, at last scaring the bear into an all-out run. Bang all the pots and pans you want and see what happens. Most black bear will look at you as if you are an idiot, and, arguably, it makes some just that much more curious, therefore dangerous.

The second story is a shocking example of bear predation and the terrible choices people make when they're in danger, which is understandable since we're so often told, "Oh, bears just eat berries and things." —yeah, right, and that's why they have two-inch fangs and three-inch claws—to better rake in those berries. Don't be so stupid to believe it. Bears are carnivores and prey on every warm-blooded thing they can get their paws on, including their own kind because they are naturally cannibalistic.

A married couple drove to Glennallen, Alaska, for a few days of relaxation in a lakeside cabin. One morning they were making breakfast when, suddenly, a black bear walked up to the kitchen window, broke it, and started crawling inside. The husband grabbed the .22 pistol that he had brought along and he and his wife ran out of the door on the opposite side of the cabin and scrambled up a ladder onto its rooftop. The ladder had been left there when they'd pulled the rain cover off the stovepipe. They threw down the ladder and at first believed they were safe, but then the bear circled the cabin and tried climbing its walls to attack them. —now here's where everything gets really weird and creepy.

The husband decided to jump down, make a beeline for a canoe on the lakeshore, and paddle across the lake for help. Taking the pistol, he dropped off the eave when the bear was on the far side of the cabin and made a run for it. He paddled across the lake to some friends of mine and asked one of them to return with a rifle to shoot the bear. What they found when they reached the cabin was horrific.

The bear had gotten the man's wife off the roof, then killed and eaten part of her. What's more, it wasn't about ready to leave her corpse, despite it being smaller than a good-sized man, and so my friend had to kill it on the spot. Everyone was incredulous when he or she heard the news, with nothing making any sense. Par for the course is what I thought, given how people are so misled about bears, particularly blacks.

Black bears, because they are so abundant, widespread, and predatory, are the most dangerous of all the species. They are sneaky, bold, timid, and nosy all at the same time, which makes them unpredictable. They are almost impossible to find when you hunt them, unless you bait them, which is no simple task because they are so cautious, yet the same bear may waltz into a campground full of people and raid their tents as if the place were abandoned. The answer lies in their intelligence, which is greatly underestimated. They are very smart, quickly adapt to different situations, and your actions will generally predict the outcome when you encounter one. You must choose wisely.

The Glennallen tragedy is a prime example of the mistakes people make when a black threatens them, even a small one. Panic ruled, rather than common sense, which would have surely saved the woman's life, and I am sickened every time I think of all the things her husband did wrong, not the least of which was to leave her behind. *Never divide your forces. Fight back!*

Why the husband didn't shoot the bear in the head with his .22 pistol when it started into the cabin is a complete mystery to me. I am not a big supporter of carrying handguns in bear country, even though I own a .44 magnum, but in this case a carefully placed shot in the bear's eye or ear would have ended the attack right there. Moreover, the .22 holds extra rounds if the first or second shot failed to make the kill. I'm completely baffled by the husband's actions, or in this case, his lack thereof. There isn't a black bear in the world that won't go belly up if it takes a few rounds in its head at close range, but let me emphasize *close*, meaning just a few feet. Anything more than that and you might as well use spitballs, since a .22 pistol has no penetration power at all. In addition, I specified the eye or ear on purpose, because that's where a bear's skull is the weakest. A .22 bullet will likely bounce right off if you shoot a bear between the eyes, where the bone is the thickest.

The man and wife should have fought the bear even if they *hadn't* brought along the .22 pistol. Both should have grabbed chairs, frying pans, or firewood and beat the bear over the head and right on the nose if they could have gotten in a lucky shot or two. If there is something a bear can't stand, it's getting smacked in the mouth. Give me two men with baseball bats and I will bet on them every time against *any* black bear, assuming both keep their wits and go after the bear with a vengeance. Bears aren't stupid and hate being outnumbered, along with getting beat to death. Trust me, because they will back off every time. Besides, why would you want to let yourself or someone you love be mauled or killed without fighting back, which is exactly what will happen if you don't do something.

A young couple was camping with their baby boy near Whittier, Alaska, one summer, only to see a black bear grab their son and take off with him. Understandably, the father ran after the bear like the Tasmanian devil, attacked it, and made it drop his boy. He stopped the bear simply with his fury, so what does that tell you. Never let a bear attack you without fighting back, and use whatever means you can to win. Assuming you have the right kind, turn your camp stove on them like a blowtorch, use a club, stab them with your hunting knife, but never, never turn tail and run. Stand your ground and let fly with everything you have, which will be especially effective if you are with friends. Again, bears hate being outnumbered, so gang up on them and give them hell.

A friend of mine in St. Paul, Minnesota kept a pet black bear for many years that he would often wrestle just for fun. *Willie* never got much exercise in his cage and ate doughnuts like there was no tomorrow, and so he weighed six-hundred pounds later in life, a big black by anyone's standards. Whenever Willie got too frisky during a wrestling match, my friend would punch him in the nose, which always sent him whimpering back to his cage. I'm not advising you pick a fight with a bear, but if you find yourself getting chewed up by one, try as hard as you can to punch it in the snout. A lucky blow might just save your life.

By now I can hear the contemptuous remarks about my ideas for dealing with bears, but let me remind you of something: *How do you suppose Native Americans dealt with them throughout a millennia? Do you really believe they went through the woods wearing bells and making all the noise they could as most folks do today? Do you really believe they fell flat on their faces and clutched their hands behind their necks as the would-be experts now suggest when one attacks?* I truly doubt it.

I had the good fortune of spending time with the Swampy Cree of Northern Canada when they still remembered their ancient ways, and there was no such thing as backing down from a bear in early times. They went after them with their bows, spears, and battle-axes, killed them, and hauled them home, because their meat, fat, and hides were highly prized. Furthermore, do you really believe that Native American women and children didn't go berry picking back then just because they might run into one? It's only in modern times the complete nonsense about bears has become so commonly accepted, as if all the bookworm ecologists know what they are talking about. I would ask you to use a little common sense and think beyond the conventional wisdom. The wildlife experts tell you to lie motionless on the ground when a bear attacks but then fight like crazy when a mountain loin attacks. *What in hell is wrong with that picture?* Like there's some way to know in a bear attack that you will only be mauled, rather than killed and eaten?

An attack in Tennessee that left a woman and her two-year-old boy critically injured and her six-year-old girl dead represents everything that upsets me with modern-day bear lore. Everyone from a newspaper reporter who wrote about the attack to Lynn Rogers of the North American Bear Center in Ely, Minnesota, downplayed the tragedy and made silly excuses for the bear. "There's only been 56 killings of humans by black bears in the past century," both said, "and disease or injury may have made the animal attack." Disease or injury, my ass, the bear was a man-eater, pure and simple, and it's way past time that people in responsible positions start telling the public the truth. For God's sake, there was more compassion shown for the bear than the poor family in one of the news articles I read. *Outrageous and unforgivable, but not all that unusual for today's journalists.* The loss of a little girl's life—hey, no big deal. "We're talking about the environment and wild animals here, and both are a lot more important than humans," often seems to be their shtick.

The mother and her two kids were visiting a campground in the Cherokee National Forest when the attack occurred. The bear grabbed the boy first, but his mother saved him by fighting back with rocks and sticks. It then clawed, bit, and dragged her off the trail that she and the children were following. Meanwhile, the little girl ran away and tried saving herself. The bear stopped mauling the mother, tracked down the girl, and killed her. A rescuer found it hovering over her body an hour later and scared it off with two gunshots. *...hovering,* what an interesting choice of words by that fellow, but I'll let you guess for yourself what it means. Anyway, the bear was never found and the campground was ultimately closed.

There had been forty-some bear sightings in two weeks in that area, yet the forest rangers hadn't closed the campground or posted any warnings. *Inexcusable...*but par for the course as I said before. *"Oh, bears just eat berries and things."* That Pollyanna viewpoint cost a little girl her life and sentenced her mother and brother to a lifetime of horror.

When will people ever learn? is my question. A black bear had killed a woman near a Smoky Mountains campground not many years before, and so how much warning does it take for people in responsible positions to see the danger, in particular to women and children? Everyone must understand that black bears live at the top of the food chain and view a child the same way they would a deer fawn, which they will kill and gobble up at every opportunity.

I have a bone to pick with Lynn Rogers and the North American Bear Center as well, since it's an advocacy group that wants everyone to believe blacks are just warm and cuddly fuzzballs that wouldn't hurt anyone. *Only 56 documented killings of humans by black bears in the past 100 years. Really?...* Okay, what about the countless men, women, and children who have disappeared in the wilds in the same time period, never to be seen again? I'll give you one guess as to what happened to most of them. Again, black bears will kill and eat you, and so your well-being depends on your knowledge of the outdoors.

I could go on and on about black bear attacks—incidents in Minnesota and a woman losing her arms near Fairbanks, Alaska, for example, but I believe I've made my point. It's time for some safety tips, and as Francis Bacon once said, "Knowledge is power." There is just one problem...well, actually more than one, since dealing with black bears is more of an art than a science. You must be able to assess risk and make snap decisions with imperfect information, although don't be discouraged because it's not as hard as you think. Planning is the key.

First, check the black bear population of the area you want to visit. Michigan, Minnesota, and Wisconsin, for example, have department of natural resources' Web pages that show bear densities and list personnel who can answer your different questions. In addition, call the appropriate forest ranger, park ranger, or game warden and ask about bear sightings. Sometimes you will be treated like a worrywart but don't let that bother you, or simply say you are a photographer who's looking for pictures. But no matter what, don't let yourself use campgrounds and hiking trails where bears outnumber the chipmunks, using the dozens of sightings in the Cherokee National Forest as a case in point, without first being put on alert. An ounce of prevention is worth a pound of cure.

Next, look at yourself objectively and decide how vulnerable you might be in black bear country. Men who are carrying a hunting rifle are at almost no risk. A lost child will become prey if he or she isn't quickly found. A good-sized woman carrying a walking stick that can be used as a sturdy club hasn't much to worry about, assuming she's not a wimp. Menstruating women shouldn't be surprised to find themselves face-to-face with a big male. Parents with little kids are in significant danger, as the Cherokee tragedy proved. Three or four hikers who are willing to go after a black with rocks and sticks are probably a bigger threat to the poor bear than the other way around. Sleepyheads shouldn't be shocked if one jumps on their tent in the middle of the night, since they absolutely love tearing up nylon, canvas, and rubber. Would-be experts have upset me all my life by warning campers, "Oh, never keep food in your tent because bears can smell it." Bears can smell food on you and your clothing regardless of what you do because their noses are so sharp. Sure, keep your food outside your tent if you wish, but black bears take after tents more often than not because it's their favorite pastime. In any case, I've given you some practical guidelines by which you can assess the risk when you're sharing the outdoors with them.

Lastly, carry your weapon of choice, which can range from a firearm to virtually nothing. Obviously, if you are camping or hiking near Sedona, Arizona (arguably the prettiest place in the world) you haven't a lot to worry about. Although there are a few blacks around there, they are too rare and runty-sized to pose a serious threat. Yosemite National Park presents an entirely different situation, since it's crawling with blacks that are habituated to people and the non-lethal policy of the park rangers. They are forever breaking into cars and food containers, to the point where there are special regulations for visitors. It isn't a good place to get careless, and Teddy Roosevelt said it lots better than I ever could: *"Speak softly and carry a big stick…"* Guns are prohibited in national parks, although government employees can carry them and, interestingly, folks are often armed to the teeth in Alaska's national parks. *Wonder what that tells you, and could there be a double standard in this great nation of ours?*

There are a half-dozen practical deterrents that can be used to stop a black bear attack, and they are a rifle, a machete, a club, a dog, a stun gun, and bear spray. Each has its strengths and weaknesses, and I suppose two or three could be used together if you are utterly paranoid, but I'd suggest that you give up the outdoors if you are *that* scared of bears. Nevertheless, let me evaluate the things I have listed.

There is no question a good marksman with the right rifle is immune from black bear attacks. Frankly, I doubt that he or she would ever have to shoot one, since I have never experienced a situation where two or three blasts from my bear rifle didn't scare the crap out of them, literally. Sorry for being so graphic, but that is exactly what happens when you have suddenly convinced one that it has made a big mistake in messing with you. You would be surprised how fast one can split the scene, often leaving its "smoke trail" behind.

Okay, so what's the right rifle? That seems like an easy question, leastwise for me, since I've spent a lifetime flying small airplanes and helicopters all over North America where

I frequently had to live and work in prime bear country. I regularly visited Hudson Bay even before most Americans knew so many polar bears summered there, and I've flown around the Alaskan Peninsula where one sees dozens of brown bear every day. In fact, Katmailand, the company that runs Brooks Lodge in the Katmai National Park, the place where people watch all the brown bears grabbing salmon at Brooks Falls (which is always shown on TV), bought my hangar on Lake Hood, the world's largest seaplane base at the Anchorage Airport. Furthermore, I can't remember all the times I've camped in Canada where black bear were as thick as fleas. My choice of a rifle is based on lots of experience.

When a wild area that I want to travel has an overabundance of blacks and people are having trouble with them, I always carry my Remington Model 7400 semiautomatic 30-06 carbine, at least if it's legal to do so. It is short, light, reliable, and noisy as hell, which are all the features I want. The Model 7400 can be bought new or used, holds almost a dozen rounds with the right kind of clip, and the ammunition (buy 200 grain bullets) is available everywhere. Considering everything, it is the most bang for the buck, no pun intended.

Granted, I have led a life very different from most people, because as a professional pilot I often found myself in wildernesses hundreds of miles from the nearest road with passengers and an expensive aircraft to look after, and so I look at bear guns differently than most people. Holy buckets, I can't remember all the times I have been stuck in the middle of nowhere for a week in bad weather or with mechanical problems. To me, my Remington is a tool that's an integral part of my outdoor gear, and I don't like leaving home without it. I've learned the hard way that if you go prepared you never get caught with your pants down, using an old cliché to make my point. And just because you carry a bear rifle doesn't mean you have to kill one with it, since you can make a good argument it can *save* a bear's life. That's always been my experience.

It's a funny thing about blacks, and it's because they have a great sixth sense. They instantly know when you're unafraid and won't put up with any nonsense. They either take off like a rocket when they see you have a rifle, or in the case of those that haven't seen a human before, they stop right in their tracks. You can almost see their minds working as they stare at you. What's wrong, they wonder, and why isn't this creature fleeing for its life? That's when I put the fear of God in them with a few blasts over their heads, which is a heck of a lot better than letting a tragedy develop like in Tennessee where people set out to kill every bear they see. Stand your ground and show them that you mean business, which is simple when you're carrying a gun. I've never had to kill a black bear in a lifetime of having problems with them. Not once.

The disadvantages of bear rifles are their weight, legality, and, most importantly, gun safety. I don't mind carrying an extra 7 or 8 pounds, but some people would rather not, and it's always important to follow the state and federal laws that govern their use. Firearms are generally forbidden in national parks, as I've said before, and certain hunting regulations may restrict them as well. A phone call to your local game warden will answer any questions you might have, so it's easy to stay informed. Gun safety is an entirely different matter, since it is your sole responsibility to be an expert with the firearm you want to carry. That means educating yourself and spending time at the firing range until you are skilled with the one you own. Don't carry guns unless you can do so safely.

I mentioned two kinds of black bear in the paragraph before last, the one that runs off when it sees you and the other that stays put and eyeballs you. In reality, there are three kinds and I always break them down as follows—the bear that's been hunted, the wilderness bear, and the teenage bear. The last two are the ones to fear, since they aren't afraid of people. To them, humans look and smell as if they might be good to eat, which portends great danger. Once again, you must remember that you and your clothing reek of food, perfume, and soap, even though you don't realize it. Both the wilderness bear and the teenage bear must be taught that you are not on the menu.

They have made it through life at the top of the food chain, so there is little reason for them to fear a human the first time they see one. Besides, I have always thought they view people as archrivals, which spells big trouble since they are territorial. They often kill their own kind and feed on them, especially if they catch a littler one on their own turf. *Now do you understand why I had so much trouble with the black bear on my gold claim?* Never turn your back on a wilderness bear (those in remote Alaska and Canada) or a teenage bear (they are about your size and weight), because it might be the last thing you do. Teenage blacks are a particular problem since, like human teenagers, they are still not smart enough to stay out of trouble.

I said before that I am not a big fan of carrying pistols as bear guns, given that it has been my observation they will likely cause more problems than they solve. For starters, most people can't hit the side of a red barn with one, especially when they believe they're in danger. For God's sake, I can't think of anything worse than having somebody waving a pistol around when he or she sees a bear. Sure, if you are a law enforcement officer who has been trained to use one under stress and regularly practices at a firing range, go ahead and carry one, but otherwise leave your handguns at home. The second issue has to do with ballistics. Most pistols simply don't have the knockdown power if you actually shoot a bear, which then leaves a wounded one. I can't think of anything more stupid or more dangerous than that.

I'll tell you a another true story to better illustrate why I feel the way I do about handguns, and it is a miracle I wasn't arrested for involuntary manslaughter and sued for everything I have. It is just too easy to make mistakes when you start blasting away with a family-sized pistol, despite your best intentions.

My wife and I spent one summer living in our thirty-foot travel trailer where friends owned an RV park on the Willow River in Alaska. I was finishing a historical series (*Whispers of the River, Whispers of the Mountain,* and *Whispers of the Wind*) for Penguin Books in New York, so I would write in the mornings and then we would fly our helicopter to our gold claim in the afternoon or go fishing, since the Willow River is a wonderful salmon and rainbow stream. *Yes, it was one of the best summers of our lives.*

One afternoon when Sharon was gone, I suddenly heard people screaming at the entrance to the park. I stepped over to the screen door of the travel trailer and looked out. The place was packed with motor homes and RVs from all over the United States and Canada and was always noisy, but this was something different. I soon learned why.

A wolf raced into the center of the park and started chasing the ducks and geese the park owner's children kept as pets. Feathers were flying, the poor ducks and geese were diving under cars to escape, and the wife of a park employee was in hot pursuit of the wolf, swinging a broom like a nutcase. I had never seen anything like it, but before I could gather my wits the incredible scene disappeared behind some neighboring motor homes. What in hell is going on, I wondered, and why is a wolf running around in the middle of a trailer park? I was stunned.

The wolf and the woman reappeared in a few moments, but this time she saw me and screamed, "Do you have a gun? Shoot it, shoot it. Help me." Ever the hero, I grabbed my .44 magnum, which happened to be all loaded and ready to go, and jumped out of the door. Now I knew what had to be wrong—the wolf must be rabid.

The wolf slowed when it saw me coming, since I wasn't more than thirty feet away. I let drive with a shot. *Kaboom!* The wolf danced sideways, stopped, and looked at me. *How had I missed?* Then not far away two little kids started running in sheer terror, and the wolf instantly started after them. I let drive again, and, thank God, hit it dead center. I walked over and delivered the *coup de grace*, because it was still trying to get up. Yikes, talk about nasty looking, this monster won the grand prize.

I'll never forget how sick I felt as I stood there. I had fired without checking my background in an RV park filled with people, one of the stupidest things I've ever done. I had let emotion overrule common sense, and it could have easily resulted in someone being killed. Leave the pistols to the pros, since it's just too easy to do something that you can't take back. Imagine how I'd felt if I'd hit someone with that first shot. I would have wanted to turn the pistol on myself.

A crowd gathered to see the dead wolf and I was treated like a hero, but that didn't lessen my self-contempt one bit. I hadn't kept a cool head, which happens all too often when one starts waving a handgun around in the heat of a battle. At the time, there was no bigger fool alive than me.

Come to find out, the wolf was a hybrid that had broken loose from its owner and gone on a rampage, which is the reason why they were outlawed in Alaska long ago. No animal has killed more children in that state, and anyone owning one needs to have his or her head examined. To that extent, I had done the right thing in blazing away with my pistol, and there has never been any question in my mind it would have attacked those two kids, and I would have been lucky to save their lives. I still shudder to think how close *that* particular horror had come.

There was a lighter side to everything that happened to me on that day, because it wasn't long before someone gossiped that I was one of Penguin's authors and wrote stories like Jack London's *White Fang* and *The Call of the Wild*. Several people took off for town and bought as many of my paperbacks as they could find, brought them back, and insisted that I sign them with the *nom de plume* of *Wolf Man* or *Wolf Killer*. What was especially funny, two elderly couples from Newfoundland had driven all across Canada and Alaska and thought it was the dullest trip of their lives. "We had wanted to see Alaska because we'd been told it was the last frontier, but nothing exciting happened until we got here. Now we see it's all true because we've seen six-guns and everything with our own eyes." I couldn't help but to grimly smile when I autographed their books. There was no use in telling them how careless I'd been.

I realize my listing of a machete as a bear deterrent will bring hoots of laughter from some people, but so be it. A person can split a black bear's head wide open with one because they're so deadly, and besides, there's no handier tool when you're blazing trail through the ubiquitous brush that covers most of North America. In addition, I love them around a campsite for cutting firewood, tent stakes, and tent poles. Easier to use and safer than a hatchet, and it's legal to carry one wherever you go, including the places where firearms are forbidden, like Yosemite for example. Now that the laugher has somewhat subsided, remember the Greeks and the Romans conquered the ancient world with a weapon very much like the machete. Look it up if you don't believe me.

I would like to claim that using a machete as a bear deterrent was my idea, but the credit goes to an Alaskan recluse named Cliff, one of the many wonderful characters I've met in the backcountry of that state. He lives year-round on Spruce Point, which sits at the mouth of the Chitistone Canyon in the Wrangell-Saint Elias National Park. Not only is this deep wilderness, but a bear infested place if there ever was one. Don't go there if you don't like getting up close and personal with black bears and grizzlies, since it's mostly thick forest laced with salmon streams. Frankly, it's funny Cliff is still alive.

My wife and I tried buying a neighboring log cabin and landing strip, which was as idyllic as could be, and spent a couple of summers working on the deal. For those who are interested, pictures of the cabin and an adjoining hunting shack are shown on pages 125 and 140 of the Alaska Geographic's volume entitled, *Wrangell – Saint Elias International Wilderness*. The sale fell through, but we got to meet Cliff. At first, he kept his distance from us, but then introduced himself when he saw that we meant him no harm. He couldn't have weighed but 130 pounds soaking wet, which generally happens when you live off the land like he does. Here was this skinny guy running around the boondocks armed solely with a .22 rifle and a machete. Good grief, I was lots more scared of his razor-sharp machete than the .22, and apparently the bears were as well. After talking with him, his choice of weaponry made sense, seeing as he could whack off a two-inch tree with a single swipe. Besides, he was so broke he couldn't afford anything else.

His philosophy behind his fearlessness wasn't all that mysterious. Bears are used to everything running for its life, so when they see some creature standing its ground they get worried. Like all wild animals, they realize any serious injury spells their doom, so they can't afford to get hurt. Sure, they might charge you, but it will usually be a bluff that will stop just short of you or veer off at the last second. That's why you must stand still and give them a nasty look that says, "Come on, buster, give it your best shot." Anyway, that was Cliff's modus operandi. Despite his diminutive size, he squared off with bears. Why bother running anyway, since bears can beat racehorses over the short stretch. Well...I suppose there's one instance where it's advisable to run, and that's when you're a lot faster than your buddies. —*just kidding!* At any rate, don't underestimate how lethal a machete can be.

Most black bear aren't very big, maybe 300 pounds on average, so anyone with a sturdy walking stick that can be used like a baseball bat can mount an effective defense against them. As you would with a machete, stand your ground and if one attacks hit it over the head as hard as you can. And don't stop hitting until you chase it off. Go at it like a maniac so it understands that you are the dominate force, which is something they instinctively understand. Bears grow up and live in a pecking order decided by size and ferocity. Other than a sow with cubs or when they are mating, they lead a solitary life governed by their ability to establish and defend a territory against all comers, although supplemented by staying smart enough to turn tail and run when they're getting the worst of it. Again, all bears are cannibalistic and therefore think losing a fight means they are red meat or that they will starve to death because they're crippled. Use their own way of life against them, which is especially easy when you're not alone. As I said before, two men with clubs can knock the snot out of any black bear dumb enough to mess with them. Don't overlook the value of a big stick as a bear deterrent, *especially* when you have nothing else at hand.

Since I mentioned a sow with cubs in the prior paragraph, this would be a good time to dispel with one of the biggest myths in bear lore, which is that female blacks will attack if you come near their cubs. That is simply untrue, and I've never understood why people persist in believing it. Good grief, game biologists regularly crawl into dens, pull out black bear cubs, examine them, and put them back. What's more, outdoorsmen have often grabbed cubs and watched their mothers race away, leaving the babies behind. The worst you might see is a bluff-charge. Female blacks aren't very big and are reluctant to get into a fight, so you have little to fear. I had an uncle in Northern Minnesota who once saw a sow and cub run across the road in front of him and then the cub became tangled in a barbed-wire fence. He stopped his car, pulled the screaming cub free, and let it go. The mother was nowhere to be seen. Enjoy the sight and don't worry about it if you are ever lucky enough to bump into a sow and her cub. I guarantee both will be gone in the blink of an eye.

Dogs and black bears absolutely hate each other, and a good-sized dog can be a powerful deterrent against an attack. The problem is most dogs aren't well trained and big enough to do much more than get themselves into trouble, which then imperils you because now it becomes necessary to rescue them. Leave most dogs at home when you visit bear country, but if you're the owner of a good police dog by all means take it along. One great benefit is that you can sleep much better at night, since it will be impossible for a black to approach your campsite without you being forewarned. I'm a product of how messed up a trip can get when a black raids your camp, and how it spoils a perfectly good vacation.

In the early 1960s, a friend and I took his father's airplane and flew into Ontario, Canada, on a fishing trip. Then a seaplane operator hauled us into a remote lake and dumped us off with a box of groceries at a tent camp he'd set up for his guests. The camp wasn't much more than a leaky tent, a fire pit, an iron skillet, and a boat and motor. But no matter, since we were there for the fishing and the lake was full of big walleyes and barracuda-sized northern pike. We were in seventh heaven... or so we thought.

We caught some walleyes for supper, fried them over an open fire, and learned our camp was pretty spartan. There was no ax, neither one of us had thought to bring a flashlight, and the only matches we had were the few I had in my pocket. Nonetheless, we enjoyed a roaring fire that night (I wanted some live coals for the morning to save on matches) and got a good night's rest despite soggy sleeping bags.

The next day we caught fish like there was no tomorrow, although we only kept two twenty-pound northern pike and some fat walleyes. We headed back to camp at suppertime, ate walleye once again, and hit the sack, since we were worn out from a full day of fishing. Unfortunately, we were in for a big surprise in the middle of the night.

I remember waking to something sniffing the back of my head through the tent's sidewall. "What's a dog doing out here?" I wondered in my half-asleep mind. Then it struck me what was happening and I have never been more scared in my life, at least not when I haven't been flying. A black bear was poking me with its nose. My scream would have waked the dead, and it surely woke my friend, since he's never been quite the same.

We both hollered and beat the sidewalls of the tent to scare off the bear, then I jumped out and restarted our campfire. Needless to say, it's no fun sitting up all night yelling and throwing firebrands to scare away a bear. As it was, it stole all our fish, which was probably lucky, since it ate its fill and finally left us alone. The next day we moved to a little island out in the lake to protect ourselves. I learned a lot about wilderness camping that night, lessons that I have never forgotten. Go prepared or not at all.

Stun guns, whether they are Tasers or handheld, will instantly stop black bear attacks, since electric shocks will scare them off every time. It really brings the "woof" out of them, and they're not easily persuaded to let themselves get zapped again. Understandably, they become terrified of electricity, and I especially like the high-powered stun pens for their size and affordability. The drawback is, other than with the Taser that's effective at fifteen feet or so, you must let a bear come in contact with you, which isn't a desirable situation at all. The stun baton is an alternative that will give you some distance, but not much. Nevertheless, don't underestimate how well 500,000 volts works as a bear deterrent.

To illustrate how well electric shocks work, I once again will mention Katmailand, the business that runs Brooks Lodge in the Katmai National Park. Katmailand also owns Kulik Lodge, unquestionably the best place in the world to fish for rainbow trout, along with all of Alaska's other fish species. Kulik sits in the middle of that state's brown bear country and its guests are continually seeing them all over the place, including wandering along the footpaths between the guest cabins and main lodge. I can't express how thrilling it is to visit this world-class lodge.

Kulik serves gourmet food to its guests, but learned early on that humans aren't the only ones who like fine dining. Brown bears were constantly breaking into their food storage, which was never much of a challenge for them because of their awesome size and strength. Finally, the staff ran an electric fence around the structure and that solved the problem. I've watched thousand-pound browns walk right past that building, eyeballing it while licking their chops, but they want no part of that fence. It has put the fear of God in them.

Pepper spray, or what's been called mace for so long, has now become popular as a black bear deterrent. There are competing Websites that sell various-sized canisters of it, and there's lots of testimonials about its successful use. I have never used bear spray myself because I'm almost always flying small airplanes and helicopters and any accidental discharge would mean curtains for my passengers and me. It's just not worth the risk, however remote that might be.

The spray comes in different potencies and not all canisters perform the same. Before you buy anything, study the various brands and make a wise choice, since your life may well depend on it. I support the use of pepper spray, but I'm not wild about it. It's often windy in bear country and the testimonials speak of the real chance of getting a dose of it yourself. That could be disastrous if you are in remote wilderness, you have just been mauled, and now have capsicum in your eyes and open wounds. And, yes, there have been instances where bears have charged right through the mist and mauled the sprayer. For that reason, read the study on the Internet titled, *Bear Pepper Spray: Research and Information*, which was written by Tom S. Smith of the U.S. Geological Survey in Anchorage, Alaska, before you start carrying the stuff. There have been cases where it actually attracts bears, rather than repels them. As I said before, knowledge is power, and it's important that you not misuse an otherwise effective product.

There is an old saying that one picture is worth a thousand words. Consequently, several must be priceless, especially when they are accompanied by a description of what was taking place. There is a testimonial on a bear-spray Website that describes an attack by a 185-pound black bear in the Glacier National Park that illustrates how dangerous one can be. Chad Adams, a passerby, stopped his car and helped rescue three small children in 2005. I urge you to look at his photographs and read what he says, then remember what I have told you about blacks. Afterward, ask yourself why the National Park Service hasn't posted these pictures on their Website with the appropriate warnings, particularly as it applies to kids. Frankly, this deliberate omission stands as evidence of what has taken place far too long. *"Oh, bears just eat berries and things."* State and national park managers must start telling everyone the truth. Black bears are cunning predators that will suddenly zero in on people when it's least expected. *Don't ever forget it because the life you save may be your own.*

HAIRY TORNADOES

I SAID IN THE LAST CHAPTER that black bears are the most dangerous, realizing lots of folks will disagree, but my claim has to do with risk management. The odds of most people running into a grizzly, let alone a brown or polar bear are almost negligible. Again, blacks are spread all across North America, and the populations in some cases, especially in certain urban areas, are increasing. People often run into blacks but won't see a grizzly in their lifetimes, presuming they don't visit Alaska or the western states, where they would have to then camp and hike in the wilds where there is a sizeable number of them. It's just common sense that you are much more likely to be attacked by a black than any other kind, since there's plenty of them and very few grizzlies. It's a simple matter of factoring.

Don't get me wrong, because I know just how dangerous the grizzly can be, but in a convoluted sense that makes them much more predictable than the black. You can almost bet a grizzly will show aggression if you encounter one, while it's hard to guess what a black might do. I have dealt with grizzles for almost forty years in Alaska and Canada and know them well, and if I have one overriding piece of advice, it's to avoid them at all costs. Luckily, since they live mainly in alpine regions, it's not that hard to do.

The problem with grizzlies is that they live a wretched life filled with infanticide, constant hunger, cannibalism, and territorial disputes. *How nasty do you suppose humans would get if they grew up in a culture like that?* Well...actually, we did in prehistoric times, and it was nonstop murder. *Now do you get the picture of a poor grizzly's life?* They have a good excuse for their bad behavior.

Grizzlies are born into a world where the big males are out to kill them so their mothers will breed again. Boars stalk the females in the springtime, relentlessly follow them, and kill their young at the first opportunity. Dominate males hate having any cubs survive except their own and know their mothers will come into estrus again in about two weeks if they're dead. It's a gruesome world, but that's how the species assures itself that only the biggest and strongest survive, or maybe I should say the smartest and fastest, since that's how the sows keep their cubs alive. Wildlife experts are averse to sharing this phenomenon with the public because it makes all bears look bad, but facts are facts. Biologists have actually discovered grizzly sows that won't breed anymore because they have lost so many cubs to infanticide, but I'm digressing a little. It's enough to say that not many grizzlies survive to adulthood, and when they do it's because they are so indomitably nasty.

Once a cub gets two years old its mother starts cutting the apron strings, and by the third year the motherly love has ended forever. It isn't pretty when mom tells junior to leave home, and the fur will fly until he gets the message. Now the real challenges begin—finding enough to eat, outfoxing the bigger males so you don't end up on the dinner plate yourself, and, presuming you have lived long enough to get big and strong yourself, cutting out a territory all your own, which means patrolling, scent marking, and defending it against all others. It's a tough job but somebody's got to do it, and besides, you get all the pretty girls if you succeed. *Now can you see why the grizzlies get so ornery?*

My purpose in limning them is to give everyone some insight into their groupthink. They attack to defend their territories, their kills, or their cubs, not so much because they are born man-killers. They see humans as another breed of bear and as they do with blacks, for example, they will attack and teach them not to come around anymore. That somewhat explains why a lot of grizzly attacks result in people being severely mauled, yet live to tell about it. Doesn't make the experience any nicer, but at least you have some prayer that you won't end up like a pork chop.

Okay, so what's the best weapon to carry when you are in grizzly country? The correct answer is binoculars. The best defense, and often the *only* defense against an attack, is to see the grizzly before it sees you. It doesn't make any difference what you use to protect yourself, bear gun, pepper spray, or whatever, if you surprise a grizzly, it will come after you in a heartbeat. The speed at which they can cover short distances is mind boggling and leaves you with almost no opportunity to pull out your bear spray or chamber a round into your rifle. Furthermore, the sudden appearance of a charging bear, unless you're utterly fearless, will freeze you in place. It takes a moment for you to react because you're in such shock, and by that time it's too late.

I would get so frustrated watching hikers in Alaska's grizzly country, since they were always simply asking for trouble. They would be bushwhacking the backcountry with bear bells tinkling on their backpacks and yelling, "Hey, bear, hey, bear," sounding a lot more like they were looking for grizzlies, rather than trying to avoid them. It was always the same old adage, "Oh, bears are just as scared of you as you are of them." Right, and that's why they will take down a full-grown caribou or moose whenever they can, just because they're such fraidycats. Don't kid yourself about grizzlies being frightened of humans, especially if you violate their space. Little bells and hog calls just won't cut it, and I'll argue that it makes them all the more curious, not something you want to do. For crying out loud, I've had to fire a high-powered rifle at them several times to get them to run, yet you want to tell me tinkling bells scare them. I really don't think so.

Sorry for being so condemning, but I've gotten really upset over the number of people who are mauled or killed by bears each year in North America. A half-dozen or more poor souls in Alaska alone and it's almost always for the lack of knowledge. You can't be taking the largest carnivores in the world lightly, which is exactly what bears are. An adult grizzly can kick the crap out of a lion or tiger on any old day, and it's no wonder because they outweigh the Siberian tiger, the world's largest cat, by a third. You couldn't get people to go blissfully hiking through lion or tiger country at the point of a gun, yet they do it all the time in grizzly country. I don't understand the rational.

On one Labor Day weekend a friend, his teenage daughter, and I hiked into Chugach Mountains of Alaska on a Dall sheep hunt. This particular hunting area was "walk-in" only, no horses or all-terrain vehicles allowed, and required at least twenty miles each way. We probably had a better chance of finding gold back there than a legal, full-curl ram, but we didn't care. September is always gorgeous with its autumn colors and cold, crisp air, and all three of us loved testing ourselves against steep terrain.

The Chugach doesn't take any prisoners, yet we were looking forward to the challenge.

I was leading by a mile or so when I spotted what appeared to be a black bear feeding on a nearby mountainside, but something looked cockeyed. The bear looked awfully big compared to the vegetation around him. I pulled out my binoculars, which I'd been using all along, and took a good look. My God, I thought, that's the biggest grizzly I've ever seen, and he's a silvertip besides, which are as rare as hen's teeth. I was looking at a record-class bear that easily weighed 1,000 pounds. He was magnificent, but he was going to be a big problem as well. We wanted to camp nearby, and there was really no other place to go.

When my friend and his daughter caught up to me, we glassed the bear for a few minutes and talked about what we should do. It was legal to shoot him, but my friend and I aren't much for killing something we can't eat. More important, we weren't carrying bear rifles, and although the calibers we had would certainly kill him, he was never more than one jump from almost impenetrable alders. That meant in all likelihood he'd get into thick cover before we knew whether or not he was dead. Grizzles of this size are notorious for the lead they can carry and still live to tell about it. This wasn't the kind of situation you want to get into with a young daughter tagging along, not if you ever want to speak to your wife again. On the other hand, unless you're dumber than a road sign you can't leave a bear like that near your campsite either. That would be just asking for trouble of the worst kind after it got dark. We were on the sharp horns of a dilemma.

We punted, at least for the time being, and climbed to the ridge top where we wanted to put up our tents, meanwhile making no effort to hide ourselves or stay quiet. We talked, made noises setting up camp, and snapped off dry firewood from a dwarf spruce. The bear was only a few hundred yards away and knew we were there, but he wasn't about ready to leave his favorite berry patch…well, not unless something better came along, like manmade food. It was a classic situation where he'd do a belly flop on our tents right after dark, a recreation that big grizzlies can't resist. *Then what do you do?* You're zipped up in your sleeping bag and zipped up in your tent. It would be the end of us because we wouldn't even be able to get our guns out. Not a good thing at all.

Just before sunset I told my friend that it was simply too risky to leave the big silvertip in peace and that we must chase him away. We then walked toward him, making no effort to conceal ourselves, and started blasting away with our rifles when we were within a couple of hundred yards. It took several rounds to get him to hightail it out of there. Simply amazing, since the bear could smell and hear us as we approached, yet all he did was go on alert. He wasn't willing to retreat until our rapid-fire shots started echoing in the mountains like cannon volleys. Only then did he decide that discretion was the better part of valor. Leave your little bells at home…or maybe carry an old-fashioned cowbell. Forgive my sarcasm, but for some reason grizzlies seem to be hard of hearing.

Once I came around a corner on a washboard road with my pickup and saw a grizzly sow with two cubs right in front of me. They dove for the woods when they spotted me, leaving me awestruck at their lightening speed, but the real point I want to make is they had obviously heard me coming for a long time. My truck must have sounded like a freight train on that bumpy gravel, yet those bear had just stood there listening. Again, making noise in grizzly country won't accomplish one thing and just makes them curious.

Back to my binoculars. Have you ever wondered why grizzlies never attack the professional hunting guides in Alaska and Canada? I know many of them because they bought airplanes from me, and not once did they ever tell about being ambushed by a bear? *Why is that?* The answer isn't all that mysterious, since they always see the bear before it sees them.

Don't get me wrong. Occasionally, a professional hunter must track down a wounded grizzly and he or she will be attacked while doing so, but that's a different story altogether. Yes, I did say she, because I've known a few women who have guided for a living, but that's getting off subject. The point I want to make is you should use the hunter's stratagem, whether you approve of them or not, since it's the smartest way to go.

The technique requires that you move through grizzly country at a measured pace, from high ground to high ground, and that you spend time glassing your surroundings. Grizzlies are seldom still and therefore they aren't that hard to spot, and that's why binoculars are your best defense against an attack by one, as I said a few paragraphs back. Rather than hotfooting it through grizzly country, use stealth to move yourself along. Doesn't mean you have to be a slowpoke, it just means you are always scouting the countryside ahead. *What are you doing out there anyway if it's not for the scenery and wildlife?* It is a time-honored way of spotting wild animals that's been in use by humans since before the Stone Age, so give it a try. One thing, though, work your binoculars in grid patterns, be thorough, and watch for movement.

Use the stealthy approach in heavy cover as well. The would-be experts tell you that grizzlies don't see and hear well, leaving everyone believing bears are almost deaf and dumb. Don't kid yourself. They see and hear as well or better than you do, but simply don't use those two faculties as much. Their sense of smell is their primary source of information, with their hearing and eyesight playing second fiddle to their noses. More important, bears are mostly focused on things close to them in wooded areas, rather than on things farther off. This gives you a distinct advantage and, frankly, you can sneak right past them and they will never know you were there, at least if you're careful. I've done it in the past.

There are two important rules that you must remember. The first is to stay downwind from a grizzly if you don't want it to know you're around, and the second is *silence is golden*, as our parents told us when we were children. We would get spanked if we didn't mind them, and chances are a grizzly will spank you a great deal harder if you break this last rule. But none of this is that hard to do.

I call my strategy for passing through heavily wooded areas "Indian hunting." There isn't a wild animal in the world that you can't sneak up on if you keep the wind in your favor, go step by step, and constantly stop, look, and listen. It requires that you watch where you put your feet and move from tree to tree, slinking along every bit like a hunting cat, and it works like a charm. It takes patience and practice, but it's not all that hard to do, and I've crept up on whitetail deer, which are as smart as they come, many times. The keys are stay as quiet and watchful as possible, and, other than when you are moving ahead, stand motionless. Most wild creatures are color blind, and they spot imminent danger by smell and movement. They won't notice you or they'll look and look and finally decide that you are some kind of strange tree stump if you stay perfectly still behind a tree or bush, even though you might not be all that well hidden. Again, practice on deer if you want to get good at it, and besides, you will find it's great sport. In addition, you will learn the woods is a busy place, and so it isn't all that difficult to sneak along undetected. You might just learn to save your life as well.

I realize that you can't go stalking through grizzly country as if you are a mountain lion, although you'd be surprised as to how far one of those cats can travel without anyone knowing it's around, but instead I'm asking for a return to the primordial ways. Picture yourself as a wolf, another predator that you never see, despite that it moves twenty or thirty miles a day, even in snow. Better yet, picture yourself as an early Native American, someone who must travel great distances through hostile country armed with only a spear and a bow and arrows, neither of which offer much protection against a grizzly attack. *What do you do?* The answer isn't that complicated, because you move from vantage point to vantage point and carefully survey the trail ahead, frequently stopping, looking, and listening along the way. You stay as quiet as possible and blend in with the trees and bushes around you. More important, you avoid the danger areas like beaver ponds, salmon streams, berry patches, and ground squirrel colonies, which all attract grizzlies. Common sense always goes a long way, especially when it comes to avoiding bears. Make like the last of the Mohicans when you visit the wilds...*although you have a big advantage over them with your binoculars.*

An attack that killed a 77-year-old woman and her 45-year-old son exemplifies what happens when people don't scout ahead. Marcie Trent and Larry Waldron were well-known runners in Anchorage, Alaska, and often jogged the hiking trails in and around the city. On July 1, 1995, they drove to McHugh Creek, a popular trailhead, and set off on a cross-country trip through the Chugach Mountains. McHugh is not only a favorite with hikers, but bears like it as well for the moose and Dall sheep they find along it. There isn't a lot for them to eat at that time of the summer and this is a prime hunting area for them. *Not a good place to make mistakes.*

Trent and Waldron had run about three miles on McHugh when they surprised a bear lying on a buried moose carcass, which is how bears protect and store their prey. Both were killed, but Trent's 14-year-old grandson, who had come along for the workout, saved himself by climbing a spruce tree. The bear then snuck off, letting the boy finally get rescued. At first, he told authorities he thought a moose had attacked Trent and Waldron, since he hadn't witnessed the actual attack, but that wasn't true at all. Both had been ripped to shreds by a bear, no uncertainty about it. Unfortunately, that particular bruin, a proven man-killer, had escaped scot-free, and no one thought it important enough to hunt it down, which upsets me mightily. Once a bear kills someone, it will likely do it again.

Frankly, I don't know where to start because there were so many mistakes made. *Never, never go running in grizzly country,* at least if you know what's good for you. Bears instantly look at you as if you are prey, except you're escaping them. How many times do I have to tell you, they are natural-born carnivores, but what's even worse is you're giving them almost no chance to retreat when you come bounding at them like some kind of runaway scarecrow. *What do you expect they're going to do under the circumstances?* It's important to remember the bear ran off once it had killed Trent and Waldron. *What do you suppose that tells you?* There's reasons to believe it would have done so in the first place if it had been given the chance.

McHugh is laid out like most mountain trails so hikers can climb up and glass the terrain ahead. Trent and Waldron hadn't done that, along with forgetting to take the wind into consideration, which are both good ways to find yourself face to face with a pissed-off grizzly. They didn't take the time to stop, look, and listen either, the three defensive measures humankind have used since we first started walking upright. People have evolved and prospered to the present day despite all the saber-toothed cats and cave bears we've faced for millennia. *Why is that?* Well, it wasn't because we went galloping through the woods wearing bear bells and hollering at the top of our voices. We've made it this far because we are smart and sneaky. Remember, grizzlies can't attack if they don't know you're there. What's the old submarine saying...run silent, run deep? It works for bears as well.

I once stopped at an abandoned gold mining camp with my helicopter to look at some old equipment that had been left behind. After circling, I landed in a small clearing a quarter-mile away, shut down, and got out with my daypack and bear rifle. It was a wonderful day but I didn't like the wind, since it would be drifting back and forth as I followed the alder-choked trail up to the mine. In reality, I wasn't as much concerned about running into a grizzly as I was a cow moose and her calf. With all the noise my helicopter had made, I figured any self-respecting bear would be long gone, but for whatever reason moose, which are only a little smarter than rabbits, often sit tight. They can come after you just as fast as grizzlies, but unlike them, it won't be a bluff charge. Not only will it be the real thing, their awkward appearance belies the fact they are as quick as cats. Moose mothers and rutting bulls are nothing to mess with, not if you want to live until old age.

Temsco Helicopters in Juneau, Alaska, once had a Hughes 369B knocked out of the sky by a moose, as impossible as that seems. The pilot and a wildlife officer had flown to Gustavas, a frontier settlement fifty miles away, and darted a cow for research purposes. Gustavus is being overrun by moose and the state is trying to figure out what to do about it. There isn't a lot of hunting around there and the Division of Wildlife Conservation wants the herd to stay healthy, but sometimes that's a Herculean task when animals start eating themselves out of house and home. In addition, it gets risky walking around town, since the moose move right in and aren't about ready to give way to any two-legged pedestrians. The city of Anchorage has the same problem and two people have been stomped to death in recent years, one at the University of Alaska and another in the suburbs. It's woe to anyone who disrespects Alaska's ungulates, that's all I've got to say.

The cow led the pilot into a place where he didn't have a lot of room and then turned on him. Why he didn't pop the Hughes fifty feet into the air I'll never know, given it only takes a split-second, but he didn't, thus the poor cow head-butted the tail rotor. There's almost nothing worse than losing a tail rotor off a helicopter, and it's a God's miracle he was able to save himself and his passenger, let alone the ship. Nevertheless, he did and now he faces a lifetime of merciless ribbing, and I can't imagine he'll ever want to have coffee with his friends or fellow pilots again. "Tell us once more how you got shot down by a moose. Yeah, right, we believe you. Uh huh, makes a lot of sense to us."

After the dust settled the wildlife officer euthanized the cow, then he and the pilot waited to be rescued. Temsco slung out the damaged Hughes and everyone went about their business, although I'm sure with endless forms to fill out. The Federal Aviation Administration never takes these kinds of things lying down, and the powers-that-be in Alaska's state government now have an additional way of justifying their existence. It's nobody's secret how federal and state bureaucracies work, believing as they do that most people can't get into so damn much trouble if they're kept busy doing endless paperwork.

Anyway, back to my mine inspection. I had a bad feeling as I pussyfooted toward the abandoned mine and I looked like a swivel-eyed thief as I followed the trail. *Something was wrong,* but I couldn't put my finger on it. I even caught a funny smell, but that didn't make much sense either. I stopped and listened as hard as I could. The brush was so thick you couldn't see more than twenty feet.

All of a sudden, there was an animal snort and the most God-awful thrashing and tearing of brush that I'd ever heard. It sounded as if the whole defensive line of the Green Bay Packers was headed for me because I had been stupid enough to call all their mothers dirty names. There was grunting, snarling, and the alder tops looked as if they had just been hit by a windstorm. I missed getting my gun safety snapped off the first time and saw brown fur coming at me through the brush. I couldn't shoot because there was nothing to shoot at, and then just as quickly the hairy tornado took off the other way. I stood there in shock, but then it came at me again. Finally, I had sense enough to start pulling the trigger—not to shoot anything but to make some noise. *Blam! Blam! Blam!* That did the trick. The bear put on the brakes and reversed course once again, but this time for parts unknown. It took me a few moments to decide whether I wanted to check out the old mine or not. I did, but ever so carefully.

The experts will argue, "Well, good enough for you, bean brain, if you had let the bear know that you were coming by yelling or rattling a tin can with rocks in it, that grizzly wouldn't have charged you in the first place." *Wrong!* You're forgetting that I'd just buzzed overhead with something that had sounded a lot like an airborne air compressor (yes, I've never seen a metaphor I didn't like). If *that* noise hadn't scared it away, I don't know what would have, short of three gunshots at close range. And I want to stress that three blasts from a short-barreled 30-06 would scare the pants off a bull elephant, let alone a lowly grizzly. You can't imagine how loud that is, not unless you've been unlucky enough to be on the wrong end of a gun barrel. It's bad enough in back, and my ears ring for a week when I fire that rifle.

I had thought about snooping around the alders to see what the bear had been doing when I came back from the mine, but then decided against it. Grizzlies are infamous for getting chased off their kills or whatever it is that interests them and then silently circling right back to where they came from, so keep that in mind when you are visiting grizzly country. Don't tempt fate unless you have to, and do what I did, and that is I looked just like the proverbial "whistling" graveyard visitor as I walked back. I was on high alert all the way to my helicopter. The most likely explanation as to why the bear was hanging around was for the same reason as I had stopped. Bears love snooping around vacant cabins and deserted buildings, much like humans, something else you should remember. For the umpteenth time, stop, look, and listen before you jump into things.

To emphasize why my bear rifle has always been such a successful deterrent, you must understand that almost *all* loud sounds will potentially stop a grizzly attack. It's been documented the hiss of pepper spray, even though the mist had missed the bear, has stopped an attack. That leaves me convinced the sudden blast of a compressed air horn would also work, although I would just as soon let someone else run the tests, not that I'm a chicken or anything. At any rate, what I want to plant in your mind is rather than yelling and waving your arms when a grizzly attacks, try clapping your hands instead, presuming you are one of those people who can do a good job of it. All my experiences have pretty much proven to me that sharp and/or piercing sounds stop grizzlies in their tracks, makes them veer off, or hightail it for the high country. Now I'll tell you why I believe this.

My greatest fear in grizzly country has always been camping out at night. As I said before, you're zipped up in your sleeping bag and you're zipped up in your tent and the wind is blowing and it's raining outside and the tent's sidewalls are pounding like you're in the middle of an Indian powwow (there I go with the metaphors again). There's absolutely no way to know that you have a bear in camp until it leapfrogs your tent, but then, of course, it's way too late to save yourself. You're royally screwed unless you can come up with a miracle. Not a good thing at all.

A few years ago, I started working on a portable alarm that would warn campers of a marauding bear, something that would give them time to respond with a weapon and/ or a deterrent of some sort. I played around with garage-door beams and motion detectors but found nothing fancy worked in the real outdoors, not unless you cleared off an area the size of a tennis court. That was not only time consuming, but in this day and age it's taboo for environmental reasons. Leave no footprint behind and that sort of thing. Finally, I happened to be fishing one day in fast water and my high-tech line snagged around something, but I still could feel a fish nibbling on my bait. *Eureka*, I thought, why don't you use the KISS approach? *Keep it simple, stupid!* I started playing around with the thread-like super-lines that fishermen have found so effective in recent years, inasmuch as they are nearly frictionless, invisible, and stretch free. Wow, was I onto something.

In the meantime, a tundra grizzly killed a married couple on the Hulahula River in the Arctic National Wildlife Refuge. I had met Rich and Kathy Huffman once and both were veteran adventurers who pretty much knew what they were doing, despite the fact they regularly challenged some of the most dangerous places in the world, namely Alaska's mountains and deadly white-water rivers.

The news media forever loves calling ANWR "pristine" and disingenuously makes it seem like a veritable paradise, although I've been there and it's anything but that. It's an absolute Siberian wasteland for nine months of the year and then for three months the bloodsucking bugs will kill you if the wind ever stops blowing, which unfortunately happens from time to time. It is a stark, brutal barren ground where you'd better bring along your winter parka and know how to survive a howling blizzard in the middle of July, and if you don't know how to swim in flood-driven rivers, overcome hypothermia, and live off the land, you have no business going there. And to make matters worse, the place is constantly prowled by grizzlies and polar bears, both of which haven't had a decent meal since they were born.

The tundra grizzly, which is found all across Alaska's North Slope and Canada's Northwest Territories and Nunavat regions, is the one grizzly that will deliberately stalk humans, at least if you want to believe the Inuit, and what they say is generally good enough for me. I have found that when Native Americans tell you something about wildlife it's usually true, and why not? They've lived here a lot longer than anyone else has. At any rate, there was lots of evidence the Huffmans had done everything right on their float trip down the Hulahula, but it hadn't done them any good.

They had at first stopped and made their evening meal, then floated further on to about twelve miles above Kaktovik, the Inuit village of 300 people that sits on Barter Island in the Beaufort Sea. Clearly, both hadn't wanted to cook and sleep in the same place, which, at the risk of being repetitious, *makes no difference at all because bears can smell your food no matter what you do!* Nonetheless, they pulled out of the river, pitched their tent, and went to sleep, sadly never to wake again. A man-eating grizzly snuck into their camp, pounced on their tent, and killed them right on the spot, giving them no chance at all to use the gun they had carried along. They had done everything right, yet everything wrong, at least in my opinion. Tragically, both had been victims of what everyone wrongly believes about bears, especially grizzlies.

Another rafter came along, saw the grizzly eating them, and hurried downriver to report the tragedy to the Alaska State Troopers. They sent officers upriver to kill the bear and fly its carcass into Fairbanks for necropsy tests, which would confirm what everybody already knew. The attack had been predatory, pure and simple. *What did I tell you in the beginning? Bears will kill and eat you if given the chance. Never forget it!*

Investigators reported that the Huffman's camp was clean and they had all their food stored in bear-proof containers, leaving everyone with the impression the predatory attack was something of an enigma. *—these are the things that always drive me crazy.* First, it wouldn't have made any difference if the campsite had been dirty, common sense would tell you that. The bear was hunting and humans are red meat. I'm sorry, but that's the extent of it, and everyone needs to get used to the facts. A tiger is a tiger and so forth and so on. Secondly, it wouldn't have made any difference if the Huffmans had encased their food in lead as if it were kryptonite, then stored it ten feet underwater, the grizzly would have smelled it, regardless. *Bears can smell better than bloodhounds, so don't mislead yourself.* Once again, facts are facts.

Let me tell you another true story to illustrate how well wild-life can smell things, and although it involves a red fox, the bear and the fox are all the same when it comes to their noses. Both are extremely smart when it comes to scenting things and their abilities borderline on the impossible. It's really hard to trick them.

My parents were dirt poor when I was a teenager in high school in the late 1950s, and if I wanted clothes or spending money like any normal kid, I had to work for it. Well, there wasn't any work where I lived in Northern Minnesota, so if I wanted to make a buck there was little to choose from, especially in the dead of winter. It came down to trapping furbearers, and it was a real no-brainer for me with mink at thirty dollars apiece and car gas at fifteen cents a gallon. I taught myself to be an expert trapper.

Mink season was always closed by New Years, so then I was left with trapping red fox and coyotes, both of which Minnesota paid bounties on at that time, plus their fur was always in prime condition and worth a few bucks more. You could get almost thirty dollars out of a good coyote and six dollars or so out of a fox. That doesn't seem like much now, but back then that was almost a week's wages, at least for a kid. I usually had more money in my back pocket than most kids in school, and I could dress as well as any of them. Like everyone else in life, I wanted to be a big shot and look the part as well, and you've all heard the sob story…life's a bitch and then you die. Well, in my case there was an element of truth in it, but I was determined that I wasn't going to live hand-to-mouth like my parents. Trapping was my way out.

The winters were brutal in those days, with snow up to your ass and temperatures running below zero for days on end, which is actually good for trappers. The foxes are hungry and it's harder for them to get around, and the one thing they do is establish trails and use their own footprints over and over again so it's easier going. I would try tricking them by sneaking up behind a log or deadfall where they couldn't see *my* footprints and slip a trap under their tracks. It's a time-honored way of catching them—that is unless you're the least bit careless and leave any scent behind, regardless of what it might be. Jeez,

Marie, those red foxes would drive me nuts with their incredible sense of smell. I was constantly asking myself, "How on earth can they do it?"

To give you an example of their abilities, there was one old dog fox that I had seen in the distance and then found his favorite crossing deep in the woods. I made sure I used a boiled trap that had hung in a balsam tree for a month and I hadn't touched anything but with scent-free rubber gloves. I snuck up on his tracks, set the trap, and backfilled with snow so he couldn't tell that I'd been within a hundred miles of him. Then as luck would have it, it snowed that night and dropped to twenty below, which freezes odors like everything else. There wasn't any way that fox could have smelled my set, but somehow he did.

The evidence was clear when I checked the set two days later. That old red had come along, gotten within a single step of my trap, and then in midair had jumped off to the side and took off like a shot. He had smelled something, as unlikely as it seems. —save your breath if you want to tell me about bear-proof containers and squeaky-clean camps, because my campsites are as spotless as anyone's and I take care of my food as well, but I never kid myself when it comes to bears. There is no way to fool their powerful noses, and they can smell things from miles away.

With that planted in your mind, I will get back to my portable alarm. Once I had discovered the amazing properties of the newest fishing lines, it didn't take me long to invent a device about half the size of a coffee cup consisting of a piezo siren, a 9-volt battery, a micro switch, and a reel holding enough "sensor" line to protect 10,000 square feet. The whole thing weighed less than eight ounces, easily fit in my coat pocket, and could be manufactured at an affordable price. Better yet, it was almost indestructible and parts of it could be used in survival emergencies, features important to outdoorsmen of all stripes. I wrote my own patent and was granted one in November of 2003 on the basis that my alarm provided the means for protecting variable perimeter and/or boundary configurations in conformity with the terrain and/or flora, which meant in much simpler terms that you didn't have to clear any land to get it to work. I then started field-testing my "PackAlarm" against the nastiest bears I could find, which, of course, are never in short supply in Alaska. Fun was had by all...or maybe not.

I saddled up my four-wheeler and headed for the hinterlands, or better said, right where I had seen the giant silvertip when I'd been sheep hunting with my friend and his daughter. Officially, this area is called the Tonsina Controlled Use Area, which has the far-flung boundaries of the Richardson Highway, the Edgerton Highway, the Copper River, and the Tiekel River. Again, it's a restricted hunting area, but in the summertime you can ride your ATV, horse, or mountain bike to your heart's content on the single trail that leads into it. And what was nice about it is, besides its abundant bear population, there was a run-down yet comfy trapper's cabin eight miles in. It was the perfect setup for testing my alarm.

It's one thing to come up with a well-chosen study area, but it's quite another to get wild critters to cooperate. Seems like every time you want a bear to visit you, there's never one around, and then when you *don't* want one there's a virtual flock of them breathing down your neck. I didn't have the time to spend all summer waiting for some light-fingered bear to raid my research campsite, and so I needed to come up with some bait. I've admitted to trapping back when it was still an honorable profession, and if there is one thing a trapper must know it's how to lure in animals, otherwise you would never catch a thing and go broke. It didn't take me long to figure out what would make every bear in Tonsina slobber at the mouth.

Alaskan Natives have harvested salmon since they first stepped foot on the place, and, of course, learned to preserve the fish by smoking it over wood fires, with alder supposedly providing the best taste. The Copper River sockeye, or red, is indisputably the most prized of the species, with people from around the world paying big bucks for each fish. It has a fatty, orange flesh that's delicious no matter how you prepare it, but one of the best ways is to cut the fish into long strips and cure it in a smokehouse. Back when the country wasn't so politically correct everyone, including Alaskan Natives, called the delicacy "squaw candy," but nowadays that's frowned upon so it's insipidly named salmon strips or salmon sticks. I wish someone would come up with a better name, "Indian candy" for example, but the point I want to make is salmon strips have a smell so strong that you can't wash the odor off your fingers once you've touched some. But what's *really* important is bears like salmon strips even better than humans do. The strips drive them crazy, and they love them so much they will even roll around on top of the stuff. I had my bait.

I rode in and set up housekeeping in the cabin, then rode ahead searching for just the right place for my test site. I wanted a location where I would get lots of action from both blacks and grizzlies, which are the two that give campers the most fits. In addition, I wanted a place that was relatively open, yet where the bears wouldn't feel threatened, which means a long way from cover. Lastly, I wanted a place where I could sit up on an isolated hill with my binoculars and keep an eye on things. *You didn't think I was going to stay there, did you?* Oh, contraire, I'm not that stupid.

Tonsina is kind of an interesting place, inasmuch as part of its access road is actually the old pack trail that ran from Valdez to Eagle during the 1898 Klondike gold rush. By 1903, it had become a wagon road with a parallel telegraph line. You can still find bits and pieces of the wire and poles the linemen had strung up along that 409-mile-long stretch, and Eagle, of course, is where Roald Amundsen telegraphed the world in 1905 that he'd discovered the Northwest Passage with his little ship *Gjoa*. There's also an original gold rush campsite back there where some trail-weary prospectors had cached enameled dishware and glass bottles in a rock hollow. The pieces were too much for me to carry as well, so everything's right where they left it. I love finding stuff like that.

It didn't take me long to find the place I wanted, and so I set up a tent, rolled out a sleeping bag I had often used (I wanted human scent involved), and stretched out my PackAlarm's sensor line in a square perimeter. Next, I built a campfire, opened a bag of Copper River "Indian candy" that I had brought along, and threw several strips into the flames, along with some bacon for good measure. Last of all, I tied the bag with the remaining pieces to a tree. If this didn't lure in bears, nothing would, and it's my belief they can smell things like this from several miles away, especially if you let it drift on wood smoke. I climbed up on my observation point and started waiting, which wasn't easy for all the mosquitoes buzzing around me. Thank God for repellent or I'd be dead.

Nothing happened on the first day, and everything was still undisturbed when I returned the next day. I was disappointed, since I thought that my make-believe campsite would get hit right away. However, it didn't take long for me to get my wish, because shortly after the sun started swinging down along the horizon (remember it never quite gets dark in the summertime) a black bear popped up downwind of the tent. It was a fat male that had been living large on the moose calves and Dall lambs it could run down, along with the rich vegetation that fills the lowlands of Tonsina. Before my tests started, it hadn't occurred to me that blacks even *hunted* sheep, but I saw it with my own eyes. They can race up and down mountains at breakneck speed, and it's all over except for the funeral music if any ewe or lamb makes a mistake. The cunning and resourcefulness of bears never fail to amaze me.

This black was cagey, because it circled the camp first at a safe distance. Finally, it made a beeline for the bait, but with its nose working overtime. It wasn't about ready to jump straight into anything. However, as luck would have it, my PackAlarm was only a few feet away when the bear bumped into the sensor line. The siren scared the bear so badly it almost did a back-flip as it reversed course, and I laughed as it tore off into some brush. It stopped, peeked back out, and tried figuring out what had happened to its well-laid plans. After a few minutes it bounded away, wanting nothing more to do with the screaming siren.

I walked down and shut off the alarm, and my only disappointment was the bear had tangled the sensor line so badly it wasn't worthwhile for me to unravel everything. However, that was a small price to pay for what had been a successful demonstration on how well my invention worked. It was clear I would have been given plenty of time to wake up and protect myself from an attack. I balled up the line, pulled down the tent, and headed home. The only sour note was the Huffmans would still be alive if they had used my PackAlarm, along with lots of other people. Somehow, I had to get my alarm into the market, if for no reason other than to save lives. I had also seen how well sudden, sharp sounds repelled a bear, which I'd hypothesized in an earlier paragraph. Regardless, I had come up with something that would let me sleep better at night.

Two weeks later I set up my test camp again, wanting to lure in a grizzly this time. My fondest hope was to attract the big silvertip that I'd seen, since it was clear he had a bad attitude, if you get my meaning. No such luck, but I'd no more than got settled on my observation point when here comes a scrawny black, which I'm sure had been waiting around looking for a free meal. Blacks and grizzlies are naturally attracted to old campsites, and both will alter the way they patrol their territories to check them every time they pass by. Established campgrounds are bear magnets, and I avoid them like the plague, another lesson of self-preservation you must learn. Go find your own campsite if you want to avoid trouble, leastwise if you can. I realize that you are forced to use the designated facilities if you visit most state and national parks, but that's just what causes so many bear problems. Those places stink to high heaven and *people* can even smell the burnt meat and fat drippings that have been left behind. How hard do you think is for a bear to smell the same things from miles away? This explains why the little girl was killed in the Cherokee National Forest. That black bear was hanging around looking for easy pickings and found just what it wanted.

The moment I spotted the little black I knew I was in for trouble, since I've said before that teenage bears are often the most dangerous. They are forever hungry because they're still unskilled at hunting, most are bouncing between territories that belong to bigger bears that will kill them at first sight, and they are still not smart enough to realize humans pose a similar threat, particularly during hunting seasons. It's all a recipe for confrontations of the worst kind, where, unfortunately, the adolescent bears usually lose. I watched with great interest as the runty black bumped into my PackAlarm's sensor line, since it would most likely be a better test than if a grizzly had come along.

This troublemaker took off just as fast as the first one did, but soon stopped and stood up. Oh, oh, I thought, it won't take long for it to decide to go back and eat the bait, then tear up my tent afterward just for spite. My North Face had cost me a few hundred bucks and I didn't want it ripped to smithereens, and that was about to happen if I didn't come to its rescue. I watched a little longer as the young bear dropped back down and circled to get a better view and wind of everything. It was afraid of the alarm, but hunger is a powerful motivator, especially for an immature, wilderness bear that has never seen a human before. It was only a matter of time before it would figure out sticks and stones can hurt me but sirens never can, or something like that. I unlimbered my 30-06 and marched downhill toward my false campsite.

You should have seen its face when it saw me coming, and it almost fell over backward when it stood up to get a better look. "Get out of here," I yelled when I was close enough for it to hear me, and that sent it racing for the woods. But I knew it was only a matter of time before it would be back for another look, which is typical of nuisance bears. Once they latch onto something, they are usually reluctant to leave, and they will drive you nuts with their persistence. This explains why darting them and using a helicopter to haul them one hundred miles away rarely works. They will cross hell and high water to come right back to the garbage dump or campground that attracted them in the first place. You might as well pack up and move away yourself, because it's unlikely they will ever leave you alone. I folded my tent and once again went home.

Bears establish territories, which I have mentioned before, and then patrol them like clockwork. Grizzlies are particularly good at this and pick specific trees for their scent markings. It's usually a good-sized spruce that lets them stand straight and rake its bark with their front claws as if to say, "I can reach lots higher than you can, butt face." Afterward, they rub themselves against the trunk, which has sticky sap oozing down, and leave a little of their hair behind, which, of course, carries their individual scent. I suspect they are rubbing specific scent glands on the tree, although I don't know which ones since I've never caught them in the act. Nevertheless, their behavior in this manner is similar to the lion, which marks its territory by spraying bushes with its urine. Almost all animals mete out scent markings in one way or another, and you should think of them as no trespassing signs.

The fascinating thing I have learned about grizzly territories is there seems to be imprecise no-man's-lands between them. I'm puzzled why these exist, but the end result seems to be certain places are off limits to everyone. For example, the trapper's cabin at Tonsina had been there since the 1950s, yet there was no evidence any bear had ever tried breaking in. No claw marks, no scats, no damage at all. The inside stank to high heaven of bacon grease, moose meat, canned goods, and a dump lay right outside the front door where everyone had thrown their garbage for fifty years. Makes no sense why it was so taboo, and talk about something that needs research, this is it.

It seems that grizzly sows with newborn cubs use these no-man's-lands the most, which only makes good sense. All try avoiding other bears as much as possible and use these places as hideouts, at least until the cubs can keep up with mom when she starts running at warp speed. It's fascinating to watch a sow with cubs when they see another bear, since they freak out at first sight. Grizzly sows are great mothers and don't take any unnecessary chances with their babies, and they will retreat whenever they can.

This is a bit off subject, but I once watched a sow with two older cubs go after a marmot that had just nosedived down its hole. John Deere would never sell any more backhoes if grizzlies could be trained as excavators, and I've never seen more dirt fly in mere seconds. I was awestruck as well at the teamwork all three displayed, and it didn't take long and it was "chomp, chomp" and the poor marmot was history. Why grizzlies expend so much energy for something that's little more than a snack leaves me puzzled, but anyone who visits grizzly country will find the animal burrows they have dug up. They literally rip open the ground.

The value in understanding how grizzlies use their territories is in how it affects your safety. For example, with all the time I spent in Alaska and Canada, it was my observation that most people were clueless when it came to selecting their campsites. Oftentimes, they would pitch their tents right beside game trails where only rudimentary scouting would have shown grizzlies routinely used these for traveling cross-country or to follow lakeshores, rivers, and mountain passes. It was a no-brainer for them to use the same routes as the caribou, deer, elk, and moose used, which, of course, are all potential prey for them. Consequently, it all worked out where campers were bitching about getting hit by cars when they had been stupid enough to sleep beside a highway. Rough terrain, thick brush, waterways, and food sources all force wildlife to use specific paths in their daily travels, so smart campers learn to read their surroundings and plan accordingly. By the way, some game trails are a foot deep because they have been used for so many millennia, so they're not at all hard to spot.

Take the wind and weather into consideration as well. I like to position my campsites so the wind blows my human and food scents out over a large lake or into terrain where I know there are no grizzlies. For example, set up camp near a precipice where the wind will carry all your odors into a rugged mountainside. Bears aren't rock climbers and don't spend much time where there's nothing to eat. What's more, I pay attention to the weather systems that are overhead, since the prevailing winds will blow one direction when there is a high-pressure system in place and then in an opposite direction if a low pressure moves in. I don't like changing camps unless I have to and always want to minimize my presence in the wilds. I'm there to see things, not to be seen.

None of this is rocket science, it's an art form based on common sense and a working knowledge of the outdoors. Grizzlies are creatures of habit, right along with people, but I suppose that's where all the problems start. We both like the same things, blueberry patches, for example, and hiking trails where the going is easier. We both like meat, fish, salads, and honey. We both pig out and pile on the weight like there's no tomorrow, then diet like mad...*but here's where my argument falls apart*. Bears have a good excuse for their behavior, since they won't be eating for several months, but fat chance that will ever happen with humans, especially these days. Guess we're not as smart as bears, but who didn't know that? Maybe we should be sending *them* to Mars, since they're a lot better adapted than we are for long space journeys.

The Glacier and Yellowstone National Parks account for most of the grizzly attacks in the contiguous 48 states, with quite a few victims being killed and eaten, information the National Park Service is reluctant to share with the public. On the flip side, your chances of being attacked fall to just about zero if you don't visit those places. It all comes down to making smart choices if you vacation in those famous parks, which then translates into staying with the crowds or employing good survival skills if you take off on your own along their different hiking trails. Once again, you must know what you're doing if you go gallivanting through grizzly country, and the consequences can be downright tragic if you don't. A little curiously, all this reminds me of the Lewis and Clark Expedition of 1803 through 1806, since that was when this nation first got acquainted with the grizzly, or as it was later named, *Ursus arctos horribilis*, Latin that schoolchildren can even understand.

The Corps of Discovery hadn't gone far up the Missouri River when the Indians warned them about the grizzly, saying they didn't hunt them with less than several warriors, and then only after all had completed the sacred ceremonies for going on the warpath. Lewis and Clark didn't take much of this seriously and all their men were eager to take on this "yellow" bear, as it was called at the time. Captain Lewis even wrote in his journal, "the men as well as ourselves are anxious to meet with some of these bear," then further remarked, "the indifferent guns which the traders furnish them [meaning the Indians], with these they shoot with such uncertainty and at so short a distance that they frequently mis [*sic*] their aim & fall a sacrefice [*sic*] to the bear."

A soldier named Private Cruzatte was the first expedition member to see a grizzly, except things didn't turn out quite like he wanted. He shot and wounded one near where Bismark, North Dakota now sits, then had to run for his life. It's not so much fun when you find yourself the hunted, rather than the hunter, and it's even lots *less* fun when you have to face your commanding officer without your tomahawk and rifle, which had been lost in the escape. Understandably, poor Cruzatte had some explaining to do, and Lewis wasn't at all convinced that he didn't have a coward on his hands. Leaving your weapons behind was no small infraction in those days, and suffice it to say someone probably wouldn't be making corporal for a while.

A few months later, Lewis would learn the hard way that he needed to be a better listener when it came to the Indians, let alone with Cruzatte, and that his impudence regarding grizzlies was pretty misguided. He and another soldier stalked two of them and shot both, but just like in Cruzatte's case, not all went according to plan. One turned tail and ran off, but the other came after them with a horrific growl and chased them several hundred feet before they were lucky enough to reload their flintlocks, fire once again, and save themselves. It had been seriously wounded by the first shot, but they were astonished to find it only half-grown, leaving them to wonder what would have happened to them had it been an adult. Lewis wrote in his journal later, "much more furious and formidable anamal [*sic*]," in comparing it to the black bear, which his men had regularly hunted after leaving St. Louis.

My favorite story about Lewis and Clark's grizzly encounters was when six of their men spotted one along the river and decided to gang up on it. They paddled their canoes ashore, strategically planned their attack, and then crept within a stone's throw of the bear without being seen. Four fired at the same time while two others waited in reserve. No fools were they, or so they thought. All the first shots hit their mark with two bullets ripping right through the bear's lungs, but that still wasn't enough to stop it from counterattacking with a bloodcurdling roar. Now the two reserve riflemen let fly and broke its front shoulder, but all that did was make the bear even *madder.* All six men then fled back to the river with the grizzly in hot pursuit. The two fastest ones vaulted into the canoes and got away, except that left the others having to hide along the riverbank and pray they would have time enough to reload their weapons. And here's where I can come in with some personal experience, because I've built two flintlock rifles from scratch that are almost identical to what those men were carrying, and I've shot both many times. The dilemma the four slowpokes faced—and it was no small one—it takes two or three minutes to pour black powder into a barrel's muzzle, ram a patched lead ball down on top of it, prime the flintlock's pan with finer black powder, close the frizzen, then cock, aim, and fire. It must have seemed like an eternity to those men as they hid in the bushes and tried reloading like crazy. *I can't imagine,* not with an enraged grizzly tearing around trying to find you, and no one can tell me their underwear didn't get super greasy.

The four who'd been left stranded started firing their second rounds at the bear, but that only let it know where their foxholes were situated, and so it charged the first two men it found. Those fellows dropped their guns and hurled themselves off a twenty-foot cliff into the river, I'm sure with the belief the bulletproof bear wouldn't dare follow them. Well, that didn't work out quite right either, for here came the grizzly with a mighty splash of its own. Then, despite being three-legged, choking on its own blood, and having been wounded by seven bullets, it almost caught up with one of them. Finally, and mercifully for both the bear and the swimmers, one of the riflemen yet on shore took deadly aim and shot it in the head. Lewis summed up the whole fiasco best when he wrote, "these bear being so hard to die reather [*sic*] intimedates [*sic*] us all; I must confess that I do not like the gentlemen and had reather fight two Indians than one bear." —well said, Captain Lewis, but it sure took you a while to come to Jesus, that's all I've got to say. Now let's hope my readers catch on more quickly than you.

At this point, it's important to note why the Corps of Discovery went after every bear they saw like serial killers, for nowadays most people haven't a clue what life was like back in the early 1800s, *especially* in the middle of an unexplored wilderness. There was no other source of fat for them, and they would die without it. They damn near did as it was, but that's a separate story. Every bear they harvested was summarily butchered, the meat saved for that or the next day's meal, and then, most important of all, the fat was cut away and boiled into an oil, which was then poured into wooden casks and left to harden into bear grease, or what we would now call lard. Bear grease was used for *everything* in those days, whether for cooking, an all-around lubricant (yes, even for sex acts), hair oil, hand lotion, waterproofing leather, you name it and it was used for that purpose. Great stuff, that bear grease, and don't leave home—or should I say—go to bed without it.

Lewis, while off by himself a month after the 'reather-intimedates[*sic*]-us-all' debacle, was attacked a second time by a grizzly, which finally cemented what he had such a hard time learning. The incident aptly illustrates what I've been preaching all along in this chapter—keep your wits about you, watch what you're doing, stop, look, and listen as often as you can whenever you're in grizzly country. Failing to do so could cost you your life, and the captain certainly came within an eyelash of losing his. Lucky, lucky, is all I have to say.

When the Corps of Discovery got within a few miles of the Great Falls of the Missouri (Great Falls, Montana), Lewis set out to survey what he believed to be a single waterfall which would only take a half day to portage. He soon learned something had been lost in the translations with the Hidatsas Indians he'd powwowed with downriver, and the expedition was now facing a twelve-mile stretch of white water that included five separate falls ranging from fourteen to fifty feet. Despite all the magnificence around him, he realized the expedition was facing an obstacle that would take a long time to get around. Nevertheless, he cheerfully marched northwestward toward the Medicine River, which joins the Missouri where it gets level again, albeit at a much higher elevation. He was happy as a clam, as they say, and why not, since he would go down in history as the first white man to see the Great Falls.

His hike upriver led him past a large buffalo herd, and so he shot one for his men who were still below the falls. He'd carry back its best cuts and everyone would then celebrate his grand discovery. *Life was good!* He watched the fat cow die of a lung shot. Suddenly, he saw a grizzly fifty feet behind him. He threw up his rifle, then remembered he'd forgotten to reload. There were no trees and the river, although close, offered almost no protection with its shallow shoreline. He was in imminent danger but kept his head and inched backward. That triggered an attack. He raced to the river, jumped in, and thrust his espontoon (a spear-like infantry weapon that he often carried) at the grizzly at the last possible moment, which stopped the attack at the water's edge. He had guessed right—the bear wouldn't risk an injury if it had to swim after its prey. It "sudonly [*sic*] wheeled about as if frightened, declined the combat on such unequal ground, and retreated with quite as great precipitation as he had just pursued me," Lewis wrote in his journal afterwards, further adding, as soon as "I returned to the shore I charged my gun, which I had still retained in my hand throughout this curious adventure. ...determined never again to suffer my piece to be longer empty than the time she necessarily required to charge her."

I'll continue my history lesson in the next chapter, and you will most likely be surprised in where I'm going with all this. In any case, I'll give you a hint. Grizzlies haven't changed in two hundred years but we have, all to our detriment, and guess who's paying the price?

THE LONG HUNTER

Lewis and Clark created a national sensation when they returned to St. Louis in September 1806 and, of course, started the opening of the American West. People couldn't get enough of the wonders the expedition had discovered, with the grizzly getting special attention. Up until then, no one had realized there was a bear that would come after you in the blink of an eye, and, to make matters worse, the firearms of the day weren't a lot more effective than using a slingshot in protecting oneself from getting ripped to pieces.

Our forefathers took all of this in stride and it wasn't long before every self-respecting frontiersman learned to out Indian the Indians, or better said, develop the survival skills necessary to keep oneself alive for years on end hundreds of miles from the nearest settlement. If the Sioux or Blackfeet didn't get you, the grizzlies certainly would, and the West was loaded with both at the time, especially along the waterways where the beaver thrived, which was why the hunters and explorers were out there in the first place. There was big money to be made by those smart enough to stay alive, or should I say, out of trouble.

In any case, do I see Jim Bridger and Kit Carson, along with the other legendary mountain men, crossing the Great Plains yelling out, "Hey, bear, hey, bear," and wearing bells on their backpacks? Of course not.

What's little known these days is there was an inveterate frontiersman who was a legend in his own time watching Lewis and Clark's triumphant return, and he was none other than Daniel Boone. Up to that time, no one had blazed more trails westward than he had, and he was still going strong at seventy-something. Talk about itchy feet, Boone was the epitome of the disease and for him to learn that he'd only made it half way across North America was more than he could stand. Something had to be done about it.

Boone had been born in Pennsylvania's western frontier in 1735 and given his first hunting rifle when he was just twelve. He had fought in the French and Indian War and then started exploring Kentucky in 1767. He blazed the Wilderness Road through the Cumberland Gap and established Boonesborough in 1775, then fought in the Revolutionary War. His daughter, Jemima, and two other teenage girls were captured by a Shawnee war party in 1776, but he tracked them down and freed the girls in an ambush. That epic rescue distinguished him so much that James Fenimore Cooper's classic novel, *The Last of the Mohicans*, is a fictionalized version of it, and he's been immortalized ever since. He had kept pushing westward and was living in what is now St. Charles County when Thomas Jefferson made the Louisiana Purchase and Missouri became part of the United States. Boone, of course, learned about Lewis and Clark's trip well before most people, since he lived so near St. Louis at the time.

Folklore has it that he often left on what were called "long hunts" and explored Nebraska, Colorado, and Montana all the way up to the Yellowstone River, which was a remarkable feat for a man his age. But he had done that back east, sometimes disappearing for as long as two years, so it's not hard to believe he'd continue with his set ways. There's an old engraving that shows an elderly Boone sitting with his rifle and dog in a western landscape, and I've always felt it aptly portrays him in his final years. He lived to be eighty-five.

The point to my history lesson is in what it tells us about surviving in grizzly country. The mountain men who I mentioned before, along with the indomitable Boone, spent lots of time living with grizzlies back when there were large populations of them. The Indians didn't usually hunt them because of the danger they presented, plus they weren't good to eat anyway when compared to the buffalo and elk that proliferated the West. The key to keeping yourself in a single piece was to melt into the countryside and keep a low profile, which was done with stealth, and, clearly, Daniel Boone was the leading expert at it, having survived two major wars and all the Indian battles he'd fought back east. Avoiding grizzlies was just part of the game, and not all that hard to do for the best long hunter who had ever lived, or maybe I should say the sneakiest.

Compare that with the constant trouble Lewis had with them, but then he wasn't a veteran outdoorsman who had spent a lifetime surviving in the wilds. His resume was mostly that of a plantation owner, scholar, and military officer, which included, although certainly not in the least, a couple of years working side-by-side with Thomas Jefferson in the White House. Hardly the best background for dealing with bad-tempered bears, but we all have to make our sacrifices. Leaving my lame humor aside, Lewis represented what we see so often today—people heading off into grizzly country without adequate knowledge on how to deal with them, which is always a recipe for disaster.

Consequently, my mind's eye sees Boone moving across the prairies and into the mountains like a cat burglar caught out in the daylight. His buckskins blend in with the background and he breaks up his silhouette with prairie topography and vegetation. He is always watching everything around him, keeping track of the wind and staying as silent as possible. There's never an Indian or grizzly that sees him first, and so they never know he's around. That keeps him in control and his destiny in his own hands, which is the biggest secret to wilderness survival. I like to sum it up best by saying, "When you feel the wind on the back of your neck, every bear knows you're there."

Just so you don't the think the early frontiersmen had it down to a perfect science and never made any mistakes, there's the true story about Hugh Glass. His legend is such that the novel, *Lord Grizzly*, was written about him, with the movie, *Man in the Wilderness*, following in 1971. No one in American history has ever shown a greater will to live, let alone better survival skills.

Glass had a colorful, if not suspicious past, inasmuch as he'd been a sea pirate and then lived with the Pawnee in Nebraska for several years, supposedly after having been captured by them but being smart enough to talk himself out of getting burned to death by having pine splinters stuck in him like a porcupine and lit on fire. *—yikes, what an awful way to die!* Anyway, it was said that he'd had some vermillion in his pockets and convinced the chief into adopting him as a son, since its bright red color was believed to have sacred powers.

Somehow he escaped the Pawnee and made his way to St. Louis, where in 1823 he signed up for a beaver trapping expedition up the Missouri River with a group of mountain men called Ashley's Hundred. Just a little south of present-day Lemmon, South Dakota, his luck ran out and suddenly burning to death might not have seemed like such a bad idea after all.

Glass was an incorrigible loner, headstrong, and fiercely brave, which is probably what got him into so much trouble. He was scouting ahead of all of the others and working his way up a wash filled with wild plums, picking and eating them as he went. Suddenly, he was attacked by a sow grizzly with two cubs (what did I say about avoiding berry patches?). Firing pointblank, he got off one shot, but then the bear knocked him down. Both started killing each other, the bear in the usual fashion and Glass by using his knife, all the while screaming for help. When his friends finally reached him, he'd won the wrestling match, but not by much. They rolled the bear off of him and examined his injuries, but as one of them would later write, "He was tore nearly to peases [sic]." An examination revealed that he had a broken leg, his scalp was almost torn away, there were holes in his throat that were blowing blood, the flesh on his back had been ripped from his ribs, there were deep wounds all over the rest of his body, and one hand had been crushed in the bear's teeth. "Old Coon," the affectionate name the expedition party had nicknamed him, was a goner, he just hadn't quite gotten there yet.

His friends sat around awhile and waited for him to stop breathing, then carried him to a cottonwood grove where they could stay hidden from the Arikara Indians who were hunting them. The Arikara had already killed thirteen members of Ashley's Hundred in a big battle, sent lots of them fleeing back to St. Louis, and wanted to finish off any survivors who were stupid enough to stick around. The problem was Glass wouldn't quit breathing and it was only a matter of time before they were discovered. Something had to be done.

An extra six-month's pay was offered to anyone who would stay with Glass until he died and see that he was buried properly. Jim Bridger, whom I'd mentioned earlier, and a fellow named Fitzgerald, said they would do it. The rest took off for the Yellowstone River in Montana.

Fitzgerald right away started working on Bridger, who was still a teenager. "Oh, I think Old Coon's dead and we need to get out of here. Let's go, kid, are you crazy?" It wasn't long before they had dug a shallow grave, covered Glass with a bearskin, and kicked some dirt and leaves over him, which, frankly, may have saved his life, since it was freezing at night. Anyway, both hightailed it out of there as well, lickety-split.

Glass regained consciousness and, boy, was he pissed, which he later claimed kept him going. Fitzgerald and Bridger had taken his rifle, tomahawk, and knife and left him with absolutely nothing. He could hardly crawl. He got himself over to some water, drank, set his own broken leg, and started wiggling like a drunken snake toward Fort Kiowa, which was two hundred miles southeast, but that was as the crow flies. It was lots farther for anyone on foot, and he couldn't even walk. He often envisioned ripping out Fitzgerald's and Bridger's still beating hearts and eating them raw.

This is clearly where the skills he had learned while living with the Pawnee came into play, for he knew how to keep himself alive by digging roots and harvesting plants for food and medicine. He chipped out stone knives, ate rattlesnakes, hid from hostile Indians, chased wolves away from a buffalo kill so he could eat, and slowly turned one mile into ten, then twenty and more. His back started crawling with maggots, but another grizzly came along, licked them off, and walked away without harming him further, which was a Godsend because it helped heal his most serious wound. Finally, he made a crutch, got onto his feet, and hobbled to the Cheyenne River, where he built a log raft and floated east to the Missouri River and then south to Fort Kiowa. Everyone was incredulous when he walked through the gate, since he looked like some kind of runty Bigfoot. No matter, because his legend quickly spread all across the West to Whites and Indians alike, which, sadly, got him killed years later. In the end, some Arikara warriors found him along the Yellowstone River, murdered him, and celebrated that they had scalped the mountain man with the big medicine, the one the grizzlies couldn't even kill. All this after he had let Bridger and Fitzgerald go free. Wasn't fair, but those were the times.

I've mentioned the Yellowstone River a couple of times, which may mislead some as to its geography. The Yellowstone River lies mostly in Montana and runs northeast across the state, whereas the Yellowstone Park, which is what most people envision when they hear the name Yellowstone, lies mostly in Wyoming. The two are very different places. Nevertheless, it brings me to something I said in the last chapter—the Glacier and the Yellowstone National Parks, or more specifically their backcountry hiking trails and campsites, encompass some of the best grizzly habitat in North America. Consequently, that's where most of the grizzly attacks have occurred, other than in Alaska. Lots of folks go backpacking in those famous places and get themselves into all kinds of trouble with the wildlife that thrives there. And I'm using the general term, wildlife, on purpose, since more visitors, statistically, are injured by buffalo than by bears in Yellowstone. Be that as it may, the strategy with dealing with both is the same. *Stay away from them!* And that's not to mention the elk, because they can turn ornery as well.

National park rules tell you to stay one hundred yards away from bears and twenty-five yards away from all other wildlife. That's not enough, and I say that for two reasons. First, world-class runners can cover one hundred yards in nine seconds, so that means a grizzly can cover that same distance in three or four seconds. *What in hell kind of safety margin does that give you?* And since buffalo and elk are just as fast, they are on top of you in just two seconds. Next, I like wildlife, and especially bears, left alone so I can see them as they're meant to be, and that surely doesn't include having a bunch of people running up to them and snapping pictures. And to worsen things, it always seems like someone has to start goofing around and taunting them, which really spoils the experience for me. At any rate, it's no wonder more people are hurt by buffalo than bear at Yellowstone. For crying out loud, they weigh a ton, run thirty miles an hour, and have never been known to be at all friendly. People are just getting way to close to them.

At the end of the last chapter I said, "Grizzlies haven't changed in two hundred years but we have, all to our detriment, and guess who's paying the price?" The point to the subsequent history lessons was to illustrate that grizzly bears have been attacking us from the very beginning and haven't stopped. Meanwhile, we've gone from the primitive Native Americans who pretty much avoided them to where there aren't many grizzlies left anymore, consequently they're the ones who have paid the ultimate price. Even Daniel Boone and the mountain men typically stayed away from the grizzlies they saw, and it wasn't that hard for them because they were all expert outdoorsmen. Besides, they weren't out there for bear and every rifle shot was a good way to bring a war party down on them, so why ask for trouble?

August 13, 1967 seems to be when grizzly attacks started gripping the nation in a big way, which has now left us with a morbid fascination in them. Two 19-year-old women were killed on the same night in the Glacier National Park, as incredible as that seems. Same day, same age, same conditions, same kind of bear, with the only difference being the considerable distance between the twin killings. *What are the chances two grizzlies*

would turn into man-eaters at the same time in two different places?
It's almost incomprehensible, yet it happened.

Teenagers Roy Ducat and Julie Helgeson hiked to a campground in the Upper McDonald Valley and pitched camp near three other backpackers who were already settled in for the night. Both slipped into their sleeping bags and fell asleep, only to wake up when a grizzly attacked them. First, the bear ferociously bit into Ducat's shoulder, pulled him out of his sleeping bag, threw him onto the ground, and sank its teeth into his legs and rear end. Next, it yanked Helgeson out of her bag and dragged her downhill into the pitch-black night with her screaming bloody murder all the way. Her cries were so piercing the people in the nearby Granite Park Chalet shot straight up in their beds. Finally, the screams faded and everyone knew she must be dead.

Meanwhile, five park employees were camping and fishing in the Upper McDonald Valley at Trout Lake. A small grizzly charged them, but they managed to save themselves by jumping into the water and accidentally leaving a backpack behind that belonged to Michele Koons. The bear walked off with it and left them alone. Later in the pitch dark, another grizzly walked up to their campfire and attacked them. They pretended to be dead in their sleeping bags until it bit one of them and he retaliated by punching it in the nose. It stood up and everyone took off for the trees, all except Michele who couldn't get her sleeping bag zipped open. She was dragged away shrieking that she was being killed.

Needless to say, all of this was pretty sensational and played well in the press, especially with most reporters wondering why the two young women had been killed when both had followed the national park rules regarding bear attacks—pretend you're dead, clasp your hands behind your neck, and that sort of thing. Of course, none of that had helped at all and the real question was whatever happened to old-fashioned chivalry. Those young women wouldn't have died if Hugh Glass had been there, that much is certain. Why someone hadn't taken after those bears with a knife, sticks of firewood, his or her fists, anything at all, Lord only knows. And then we are left to wonder what would have happened had one of them had a machete and guts enough to use it.

Unfortunately, there had been no one around to help Brigitta Fredenhagen with any kind of weapon or anything else. In July of 1984, Yellowstone Park rangers noted that she hadn't reported back from a solo hike in the White Lake area. They searched for her and found her tent flattened and ripped open, with her partially eaten body about 250 feet away. There really weren't any signs of a struggle, and she had bear-warning pamphlets and bear bells with her, plus she'd hung her food some distance away from her tent, but to no avail. She did have a chocolate bar and some other stuff in the tent, but nothing that would really explain why the bear hadn't gone after her food cache first. Park officials ultimately decided she shouldn't have been camping alone, which is something they discourage. I've already told you how bears feel about tents, let alone the people in them, so we won't go into that again. Suffice it to say, you take your life into your own hands if you go camping in grizzly country without some way of protecting yourself. Now let's ask ourselves what would have happened had she had a stun pen along and zapped that bear with 500,000 volts, especially when it was pretty obvious she'd tried playing dead and paid the price for being so foolish. I'm one who would bet she'd still be alive.

Most people can't imagine fighting a grizzly and seem inexplicitly willing to forfeit their lives. Somehow they've bought into the silly idea that if they lie down, curl up, and play dead they will survive an attack, which defies common sense. The *least* that will happen is they will be left with live-threatening injuries that will require hospitalization, and that's only if they get lucky and aren't killed outright, but no one has any way of knowing the final outcome of an attack until it's too late. What is everyone thinking? *"Oh, now I see that I should have fought back, but it really doesn't matter because I can always come back from the dead."* None of the existing groupthink makes any sense to me. You must stand your ground and fight like there's no tomorrow, since that's probably the case, rather than leave everything to pure chance.

Chris McLellan did just that on August 15, 2007, which undoubtedly minimized his injuries and saved him from certain death. His deadly encounter with a sow grizzly and three cubs in an oat field near Grande Prairie, Alberta, stuns me, since it was one of my favorite gas stops when I was flying my airplane and helicopter between Arizona and Alaska, and it's all pretty much farmland. It never occurred to me there were grizzlies living there, which apparently was McLellan's problem as well, since he had just moved from Nova Scotia.

Chris drove into the countryside, stopped at an oat field, and got out to scout for a place to bow hunt deer. He started through the oats with only his hunting knife and a digital camera, then saw a sow grizzly with three cubs rear up when he was only a couple of hundred feet away. He yelled and waved his arms, thinking that would scare them off, but the sow came at him like a wide-open ATV. Next, he tried flashing his camera in the hope that would stop the charge, but it wouldn't go off. He pulled out his knife, which, luckily for him, had a foot-long blade, and lifted it above his head.

The bear hit him going full blast, grabbed his left forearm in her teeth, and both hit the ground hard. He started stabbing her in the neck with his hunting knife, and she let go and bit his body and right arm. Then, all of a sudden, she stopped her attack and walked away, letting him get back onto his feet. He limped out of the field, found a farmer who called emergency, and an ambulance raced him to a hospital where he underwent surgery for a broken left forearm and his other injuries. The bear was found dead the next day, which doesn't surprise me after being stabbed in the neck several times with a long, sharp blade. I'm reminded of *Crocodile Dundee* when he said, "...*this is a knife*," after he'd pulled out his old-fashioned Bowie knife.

McLellan had made some mistakes, which contributed to the attack. First, it seems he ventured into grizzly country without realizing it, and then compounded the problem by not taking the time to stop, look, and listen as I've constantly preached. The attack wouldn't have taken place if he'd gotten up on higher ground and glassed his surroundings, plus there would still be a valuable grizzly left alive. Their populations are increasing and spreading across the West, and that's fine with me, but we all must change the way we use the outdoors so we minimize the dangers. The only answer is in our ability to become better outdoorsmen, which is why I told the stories about Daniel Boone and Meriwether Lewis. Clearly, we've lost our wilderness skills to the glitz and glimmer of modern life, and so we must reeducate ourselves.

Photographer Jim Cole's two brushes with death give emphasis to my point, given that he's the only person I know who has been mauled twice by grizzlies. Interestingly, my wife remarked, "He got what he was asking for," when she first read about him in the newspapers, and since I trust her insight into most matters, I agree. Even the National Park Service thought he was pushing the limits too far and had him hauled into court to prove their point. It didn't do any good.

Cole is an author and a commercial photographer from Bozeman, Montana, who has often worked in the Glacier and Yellowstone Parks taking photos of grizzlies. In 1993, he and a friend got too close to a small grizzly in Glacier and it attacked them, which landed Cole in the hospital with a broken wrist and assorted wounds. Fortunately, his companion rescued him with pepper spray. Later he would write, "I figured this was as traumatic an experience for the young bruin as it was for me." Regrettably, that's the same old nonsense that's been used for ad nauseam about bears being just as scared as you are. Let me assure you that grizzlies don't get any more traumatized than the Aryan Brotherhood does after they nearly beat someone to death. Neither is much into remorsefulness, if you get what I mean.

Finally in 2004, the Park Service had had enough of Cole creeping up on bears and ticketed him in Yellowstone for getting too close to a grizzly sow with two cubs. He beat the rap in court, which is no big surprise. Just who among us wants to run a tape measure between a bear and a photographer so the facts are straight? *Not me!*

And this is where my wife comes in, since she's taken lots of bear pictures, especially in Alaska's Denali National Park, which is America's Serengeti. She'd win a drawing every year that would let her drive her own car into the park to photograph the "big five," the caribou, Dall sheep, grizzlies, moose, and wolves that populate the place. Her comment about Cole getting what he asked for was based on her personal experiences, including her observations of all the other wildlife photographers who would visit Denali every fall after the park had officially closed. It's a bit of a gold rush, and you can read about it on the Denali National Park Page under "Road Lottery." Trust me, it's a once in a lifetime trip.

The park lets 400 cars drive in on its single access road for four days each September, which gives hundreds of photographers an opportunity they would otherwise never get. You can imagine the hordes that take off after the wildlife they see when there aren't any park rangers around to stop them. My wife laughs every time she remembers jogging across the tundra right along with everybody else, each carrying his or her tripod as if he or she were on some kind of infantry charge. Of course, when someone would spot a park ranger coming down the road in a government pickup, the horde would freeze and everyone would pretend he or she had been standing there all along and the moose, wolf, or bear had walked up to him or her, not the other way around. There's this old photographer proverb that says you must get close enough to catch the glint in the animal's eyes, and I'll let you guess how close that might be.

On May 23, 2007, Cole was attacked a second time by a grizzly, this time in Yellowstone along Trout Creek in the Hayden Valley. He was off by himself taking pictures and apparently saved himself by using the pepper spray he was carrying. After walking about three miles to the Grand Loop Road, passersby called for help and he was flown to Idaho Falls by helicopter for emergency care in a hospital, where he was hooked up to a ventilator and a feeding tube. Clearly, he was lucky to be alive, since the bear had gone after his head and face with its teeth and claws.

Craig Dahl wasn't so fortunate in May of 1998. He was a 26-year-old from Winter Park, Colorado, who had just started working at the Glacier National Park as a bus driver. Along with everyone else, he'd attended a lecture that had described the job-related risks he'd be facing, which included strict warnings about the bears that lived in the park.

Craig disappeared after he'd hiked off on his own to the Two Medicine Valley, a remarkably rugged and beautiful part of Glacier. Two days later, the park rangers began their search of that particular location and what they found was one of the most shocking episodes in national park history. They quickly called the local sheriff to come out for an investigation, and as he completed his on-site search, several men stood in a perimeter with 12-guage shotguns. "They were there protecting me and my crew so we wouldn't get jumped by the bears coming back to defend this area," he said afterward.

Craig's glasses were discovered on top a steep, rocky slope and shreds of his clothing trailed down to a tree line where grizzly hair and scat were scattered about. Two hiking boots with his feet still inside were lying nearby, along with some bits and pieces of fabric. "All that was left of this body was a few bigger bones, skull, and a small piece of skin," the sheriff explained. "In my initial investigation, it looked to me like this person was mauled, killed, and eaten by a grizzly or grizzlies," he added. The body remnants were retrieved, along with the grizzly hair and scat, so an autopsy and DNA tests could be run. Although Craig's billfold and keys had been found, they wanted to be absolutely sure.

Not long afterward, a 13-year-old sow grizzly named Chocolate Legs, along with one of her twin cubs, were shot and necropsies performed. DNA tests proved that she and her cubs had eaten Dahl, and so it was presumed they must have been the ones that had killed him as well. The second cub was never found. Glacier's superintendent said later, "Although we cannot prohibit people from hiking alone, we strongly discourage it. Glacier National Park is a wild place, but there's safety in numbers." The Park Service decided that Craig had surprised the bears, tried running, and that had been the end of him.

Unfortunately, as the Dahl story proves, there is no surefire way to guarantee that you will ever survive a grizzly attack if you're unlucky enough to face one. They are very aggressive by nature, powerfully built, lightning fast, and to make matters worse, the supposed experts have continually disseminated safety tips that are unproven at best, along with being mostly illogical when you think about them. The litany includes, "don't look directly at bears, bend your knees and make yourself look smaller, talk softly, don't carry smelly food and keep its odor off your clothing, although burn your garbage and pack it out with you." *—my God, why don't you just set up a bait station on wheels, since that's what you've just become?"* The naivety behind most bear tips is disturbing, and I've already written about their sense of smell, but to be more specific, it's probably a thousand times better than that of a human's. Nowadays, most bear safety tips are meant to be environmentally friendly and politically correct, rather than germane to keeping people alive.

It all boils down to maintaining an acute awareness of your surroundings when you're in grizzly country, the judicial use of binoculars to survey the cross-country trails you want to use, and the development of your ability to sneak along without being detected. Remember, your goal is to see grizzlies before they see you.

# THE TERRIBLE TON

PICTURE A BEAR THE SIZE OF A PLAINS BUFFALO and you have the Alaskan brown bear. Wait a minute, you say, buffalo weigh more than a ton, so that doesn't make sense. Well, just so you know, it's said that one from Kodiak Island tipped the scales at 2,500 pounds. What's more, the same kind of bear can run as fast and far as a horse. I once watched a huge boar at Bear Lake chase another for two miles up and down the mountainsides just south of the lodge I mentioned in an earlier chapter. Their size, power, and endurance are beyond belief, and it's no wonder they can snap a moose's neck with their fangs and forepaws in a matter of seconds.

There is a universal fuzziness among wildlife experts regarding the differences between brown bears and grizzlies, so now most claim both are the same species. They will, however, point out the bear on Kodiak Island are a separate subspecies from the rest of Alaska, inasmuch as their skulls and genetics are a bit different than their buddies over on the mainland. This, of course, is because of the Kodiak bears' longtime isolation. Regardless, it doesn't take too many brains to figure out that comparing an Alaskan brown to a Montana grizzly is like comparing a Hummer to a Harley.

Big game hunters have always wrung their hands regarding what constitutes a brown versus a grizzly, since they want it to go into the books as a record-class specimen when they kill one. Somebody a long time ago came up with the harebrained idea that if you shoot a brown within 75 miles of Alaska's coastline it's a brown and if it's one farther inland it's a grizzly. Even at first glance, this doesn't make a lot of sense. For starters, Alaska's coastline looks like an unfinished jigsaw puzzle, so where do you draw the line, and then to top it off, all male browns think nothing of taking off across hill and dale every spring to hook up with a new sweetheart. Consequently, there's been more than one 400-pound female grizzly that's been knocked up by a 1,200-pound boyfriend, and humans aren't the only ones who have unplanned pregnancies. There's a little cohabitation going on out there, which probably explains the humongous silvertip I saw in the Tonsina walk-in area. The species *Ursus Arctos* has gotten somewhat blurred over time.

We all think brown bear hibernate just like blacks and grizzlies do, but there's an interesting difference between them, inasmuch as it's rather normal to find a brown wandering around in the middle of January, particularly down on the Alaskan Peninsula or on Kodiak Island. Why this happens, no one really knows, and for some odd reason wildlife biologists don't seem much interested in spending a whole winter with a 1,500-pound brown to find out. Go figure.

Actually, someone on the Kamchatka Peninsula tried and paid with his life, so maybe that has something to do with it. And what's so sad about it, the guy, of all people, should have known better. It's the old story, familiarity breeds contempt.

Vitaly Nikolayenko had spent twenty-five years following and photographing Russia's brown bears. He was a self-educated bear expert who kept detailed records about their behavior and had even gotten international attention for his devoted work, including a visit from the *Los Angeles Times*, seeing as they hadn't yet come to grips with the predation of Timothy Treadwell and Amie Huguenard. Hollywood has never wanted to admit that bears can turn into man-eaters and what better way to sell the idea they are actually nothing but misunderstood house pets than to write about someone who had worked with them for a lifetime without getting hurt. Besides, Tim and Amie had only been dead for a couple of months, so bear stories were still red hot.

Just before Nikolayenko was to join his wife for their 2004 New Year's celebration, he trailed a midsized brown to a small lake a short ways from his one-room shack on the Tikhaya River in the Kronotsky Wildlife Reserve. The tracks in the snow told everyone what had happened next.

He had crawled into some brush after the bear to get some close-up pictures. The brown had gotten out of its bed and killed him, despite the clear evidence of orange pepper spray having been aimed right at it. An unfired flare gun lay nearby as well, along with a broken and bloody camera. His body had been half eaten, despite the capsicum that must have contaminated both the bear and Vitaly himself. So much for the reliability of bear spray as a surefire defense, although the *real* story is he'd been following bears far too long and finally paid the price for it. There's no question that particular bear knew him and had gotten upset about being relentlessly shadowed. Like I said, familiarity breeds contempt, especially with bears.

Brown bear mostly den where you really wouldn't expect them to, and that's up on the mountainsides where they can settle themselves in hollow spaces and let the snow drift over them. Some use natural caves and a few find holes in the lowlands big enough to crawl into, but for the most part they hibernate in beds next to the mountaintops. It's my belief they not only understand the insulating qualities of deep snow, but also that the coldest winter air sinks into the bottomlands and leaves the higher elevations a little warmer. It's fairly evident as well they use their denning areas over and over again, which only makes sense since they tend to be so territorial.

All bears rely on their fur coats to keep them alive through the long winter months, and browns are no exception. The temperature inside their dens, along with any other species of bear, isn't much warmer than the outside air, so it all comes down to the bedding they've raked together, the way they curl up to fend off the cold, and the effectiveness of the shelters they've chosen to protect them from the wind. Otherwise, it's all a matter of the specialized physical gifts Mother Nature has given them, which is no less than miraculous.

Bears can flip their switches on and off all winter long, meaning they can intentionally manipulate their heart rates, recycle their urine, and stop defecating. In the meantime, they turn their summer fat into lifesaving fuel, which means they will lose about one-fourth of their body weight by springtime. Bears are unique in their ability to sustain themselves, and they don't hibernate quite like any other animal.

They occasionally wake up from hibernation during the wintertime, either because they've been disturbed in some way, or in the case of a female, they've just given birth and are nursing cubs. This accounts for a lot of the hair-raising stories about people finding a frosty tunnel in a snowdrift and getting the nastiest surprise of their lives when they peek inside. "Hey, Harvey, what-d'ya suppose this big hole is for?" only to find themselves face-to-face with a grizzly that's hopping mad about getting woken up before springtime. What's the old saying, curiosity killed the cat?

An incident something like this almost cost an Alaskan hunter his life. In April of 2007, Lynn Keogh and his hunting buddy, Ray Bendixen, were snowmobiling in the mountains between Glennallen and Talkeetna when they spotted a grizzly lying just outside of its den up on a brushy hummock. They glassed the bear for several hours and made sure it was a legal trophy and not a sow with cubs. They made their stalk and Lynn shot it, then both rode their snowmobiles almost up to the kill site. It was a magnificent spring day and Lynn posed beside the grizzly for some pictures. Little did he know he was about to get the shock of his life.

When he started dragging the dead grizzly away from the den's entrance so he could skin it, he heard a bloodcurdling roar. He lunged for his rifle and got off one shot, but then it was too late. Another grizzly knocked him down and began biting him from head to foot. On his legs, his side, his shoulders, and then it went after his head. He could hear the bear's teeth crunching on his skull, and he put up his hands and got those bitten as well. Then the bear and he somersaulted down the mountainside.

Ray Bendixen made a dive for his snowmobile, which was parked a few yards away, and grabbed his rifle. Thank God he was a crack shot, because he saved Lynn with three well-placed shots. It's no small feat to hit a moving target, and it doesn't help at all when you know it means your friend's life even if you miss by a couple of inches. The man's a hero in my eyes, and I wouldn't want to try making those shots. What's more, he saved the day with a .220 Swift, which is nothing more than a souped-up jackrabbit rifle. Godalmighty, was Lynn ever lucky to have him along.

They used a satellite telephone to get an emergency-rescue helicopter to ferry Lynn to an Anchorage Hospital where he was treated for his wounds, which included the use of staples on his head. The next day, it was learned that his single rifle blast had almost penetrated the full length of the second grizzly just before he'd gotten knocked down, but it hadn't stopped the charge. And what's amazing, the shot had come from a .338 at pointblank range, which is a cannon-like rifle that's often used in Africa on dangerous man-killers such as the Cape Buffalo and the hippo. Goes to prove that carrying a bear rifle is no guarantee you will survive an attack.

The brown bear that leave their dens in the middle of the winter are called "beach bears," since that's where they are most often found. They are typically the smaller ones that haven't gotten good at fattening up because of the fierce competition at the salmon streams and their ability to hunt isn't all that well developed either, so they're out looking for an easy meal. All winter long, dead walrus and whales wash up on shore, along with the possibility of them finding a seal that's gotten a little too stupid. Everything is fair game, and they will feed on seaweeds as well. Alaskan tidelands are bountiful places and lots of good things are left high and dry.

This phenomenon of brown bear wandering around in the dead of winter has given rise to what's sometimes called the "ice bear," which has resulted in the sad demise of more than one old-time trapper or gold prospector. The Alaskan Peninsula and Kodiak Island are infamous for their freezing rains that cover everything with sheet ice, which includes the fur of any brown bear caught out in it. Now you have a hungry 1,000-pound bear and it's suddenly spotted something walking around on two legs that might make a tasty meal. Big browns are dangerous enough as it is, let alone the fact they are now covered with armor plating solid enough to deflect a bullet. It all makes for a very nasty situation, and there's been any number of Kodiak townspeople who have asked in the past, "Wonder whatever happened to old Wilbur, because he always came into town at Christmastime?" An interesting sidebar to this is that one-fourth of the island's bears never hibernate under any circumstances, which means you never know when you might run into one. The second thing that's an enigma with Alaskan browns is their ability to recognize what gunshots mean. It brings them in at full gallop, much to the horror of the hunter who has just killed a deer or an elk, or has been foolish enough to take a pot-shot at something just for kicks. Nowadays, most deer hunters in Prince William Sound and on Kodiak Island, or on Admiralty, Baranof, and the Chickagof islands in Southeast Alaska carry what would make half-decent elephant guns just for that reason, rather than the typical peashooters one would use on the pint-sized blacktails that inhabit those places. Humans aren't the only ones who love venison.

Gene Moe, an Anchorage cement contractor, learned that the hard way on November 1, 1999, but true to his reputation he survived, despite his body looking as if it was covered with funny-looking zippers after the surgeons stitched him back together again. He had always been a tough hombre, earned in part because he'd once pitched off a mountain, tumbled several hundred feet, and lived to tell about it. Alaskans take great pride in their near misses and Gene is no exception, although he credits his exceptional courage to God, country, and love of his family. Regardless, not many 68-year-old men could do what he did one November night.

He was deer hunting with his son and two old friends on Raspberry Island, which lies just north of Kodiak Island, when he finally shot one right at sunset. He started butchering it so he could get back down to the beach and join his hunting party before it got pitch dark. Raspberry is rugged and covered with high grass, alder shrubs, and Sitka spruce, so it's easy to get lost or take a nasty fall when you're packing out a deer. Bent in half, he was hurrying with his knife.

"Arrrrrrrrrr...!"

Instantly, Gene knew he was in big trouble, especially since he'd left his rifle a few feet away. The brown hit him like a freight train, bit his arm, and knocked him flat. All he could do was kick the bear with his hunting boots. He let drive with every bit of his strength and flipped the bear off to one side. Next, he jumped back onto his feet and got ready with his knife.

The bear charged him again and both went after each other without mercy. Blood started spurting everywhere. Every vicious bite was answered with a deadly stab, and it was a fight to the death. Finally, the bear backed off and circled a few feet away, and Gene waited for it to come in for the final kill.

The bear made another lunge for him and he punched it in the nose with a flying left hook, which luckily knocked it headfirst into the ground. He stumbled over to his rifle and, despite his broken and bleeding hands, fired three times as fast as he could. Immediately afterward, he realized he would surely bleed to death if he didn't get help. He headed for a familiar mountain on nearby Afognak Island as if it were a heavenly beacon, since it would lead to the nearest beach and maybe his son or one of his friends. There was no time to spare.

He lay down a few times to die, but his secret voice screamed for him to get up and keep going. It was almost like freezing to death where one simply wants to sleep. He fought his way downhill almost two miles until he finally made it to the beach, where he found his hunting partners wondering what all the fireworks had been about. It took only one look and they instantly knew, so they administered as much first aid as they could, got him into a boat, and set off for a fishing lodge where they could get further help. The U.S. Coast Guard flew in with a helicopter and took him to the Kodiak hospital where he underwent reconstructive surgery, which included several hundred stitches. A long strip of leg muscle was flopping loose and shredded flesh and skin hung from his arms and shoulders. Just as it had been with Hugh Glass, "He was tore nearly to peases [sic]."

In the meantime, 53-year-old Ned Rasmussen wasn't so lucky over on Uganik Island, a mere ten miles away. It took two days for searchers to find his body hidden in an alder maze at the foot of a long ridgeline, not far below from where his rifle, cap, and some blood had been found. His hunting partners had last seen him in that general vicinity and they'd also heard a single shot, which they assumed meant he'd gotten a deer. Little did they know the worst thing possible had taken place, especially since he'd hunted the island for fifteen years and was well aware of its dangers.

A rescue helicopter had spooked a wounded sow with cubs while it had searched for him and everyone started putting two and two together. His fatal wounds were consistent with an attack, except he'd survived at first and tried walking down to the U.S. Forest Service cabin he and his friends were renting. He simply hadn't made it, since the trauma had been too much for him and he'd bled to death or died of shock. The fact is that not many people are tough enough, let alone lucky enough, to survive a brown bear attack, as they are just too big and powerful. Separation is the key to your survival, and you must stay away from them. The alternative usually promises a slow and painful death.

The Alaska Department of Fish and Game instantly blamed weak salmon runs, poor berry crops, and the winterkill of deer for the attacks on the two men. The problem with that picture was there had been no closures of commercial fishing, let alone sport fishing, around Kodiak Island at the time, so the story of weak salmon runs doesn't make a lot of sense. And why were there deer seasons being held where multiple animals could be taken if the deer were so devastated and bears were subsequently starving? Last of all, it's ludicrous by any stretch of the imagination to suppose brown bears depend on the success or failure of berry crops just so they won't prey on humans. Browns simply don't behave that way.

I don't mean to be critical of the Alaska Department of Fish and Game, and since I've sold airplanes and helicopters to its different officials in the past, I know about the pressures they come under, especially when the *Anchorage Daily News* starts questioning them about bear attacks. It runs from the opportunity to get their names in the paper to telling the newspaper reporters what they want to hear just so they can just get rid of them. *Let's face it, there's no way of knowing exactly why brown bear attack people.* They aren't talking, and we probably wouldn't listen to them even if they decided to start. It doesn't matter anyway, since common sense gives us the answer, except nowadays most people don't want to listen to it. *Brown bear are by far the world's largest meat eaters—always have been and always will be, and it's all part of nature's plan.*

For some strange reason modern-day man has decided that brown bears are actually born-again vegetarians, rather than the biggest predators on the planet. It all has to do with environmentalism, the green agenda, anti-hunting, Smokey Bear, bear viewing, and maybe some things I've forgotten. Whenever they are shown on TV, they're grazing like cows in green pastures, or in the worst case, eating salmon like finicky cats. We are never, ever shown pictures of them pouncing on caribou or moose calves while the poor things are helplessly bleating because they're being eaten even before they've had the chance to die. And meanwhile their frantic mothers are running around in circles and moaning animal sobs because there's not a damn thing they can do about it. Let's just say the Disney crowd has overdone their work, and thus we've been given a false picture of Mother Nature and where the brown bear fits in. For that reason, let me give it to you straight a second time—they were put here to kill and eat things, humans included.

Several years ago, a few dozen tourists got a firsthand lesson in brown bear biology at Brooks Falls in the Katmai National Park, and I doubt that any one of them will soon forget what they saw. Let's just say, sometimes Ma Nature can be a little too bloodthirsty for most folk's taste.

Once again, Brooks is where scores of browns show up every summer for their yearly salmon feast, and it's normal to see a dozen or more there at any given time. I doubt there's another place in the world where tourists are left to wander around in a Jurassic bear sanctuary with the real opportunity to literally bump into one. It's a wonderful, once-in-a-lifetime experience and the actual source of almost all the brown bear pictures you see on TV and in glossy magazines. It's open to absolutely everyone, don't forget your camera, and jack up your courage, since there's nothing at all to prevent a hungry brown from breaking its traditional fish diet and eating you. I guess that's why the place is so special.

Alaskan seaplane pilots fly people into Brooks Camp, the Katmai National Park headquarters on Naknek Lake, and drop them off for their one-of-a-kind trip, which can be a single day or overnight if you were smart enough to make reservations for a room, which should be done a year or two ahead since the place is always so busy. Once you step off the plane, you must attend a safety briefing that tells everyone what the rules are regarding the walking trails, viewing platforms, camping out, carrying backpacks, food storage, and fishing, if that's what you chose to do. Basically, the rangers insist the bears be left alone and given the right of way. Live and let live—behave yourself and you won't get slapped with a fine. "Okay, but what happens if the bears misbehave?" you ask. Well, they get shot at with whizbangs and rubber bullets, so which would you prefer?

One of my favorite bear stories is once upon a time the Katmai rangers briefed a young couple about brown bear safety and then let them loose to explore the wonders of the Brooks Falls. The couple got part way down one of the walking paths by calling out, "Yo-ho, bear, yo-ho, bear," and carefully watching all around them. Suddenly, a big brown stepped out right in front of them and now it was time to practice the safety tips they'd just been given. The young man scurried off into the trees to let the bruin pass by unchallenged, which is what he'd been told to do. He then looked back for his wife, only to find her somewhat confused about what they'd just been taught. She had taken the "lie-down-and-play-dead" part a little too seriously and was curled up in the middle of the trail from whence he'd just come. The big brown walked up, sniffed her, and laid down beside her, evidently deciding it was, indeed, a nice place for a nap.

The tourists I mentioned three paragraphs back were all ogling the ever-present brown bears from the viewing platform at Brooks Falls when a good-sized boar decided on a change in fare. It saw a sow get a bit too careless with a yearling cub and took the opportunity to kill it and carry it to the foot of the stand, where it proceeded to eat it in ghoulish fashion. Most of the tourists now wanted to leave, but the ranger who was running the stand knew that probably wasn't a good idea, since the boar might decide they all wanted to steal away his yummy meal. Mr. and Mrs. Average American got a real lesson in bear behavior that day, since eat or be eaten is the fundamental law of their lives.

The employees at the Greens Creek silver mine on Admiralty Island got a graphic lesson on bear cannibalism as well. In the summer of 2006, they were stunned to see a small brown zip through their work yard, followed by a bigger one not far behind. Back and forth both went, dodging between the metal buildings, pickup trucks, and heavy equipment sitting next to the mine's underground operations. Clearly, the smaller bear was hoping to scare off its attacker by using the presence of humans and their noisy activities, but it wasn't working. Finally, the larger brown caught up, killed the littler one, and ate part of it. Once the killer had finished its meal and left the area, the maintenance crew hauled off the remaining carnage with a front-end loader and hosed everything down to get rid of the blood, no doubt a little chastened by what they had just seen. *There but for the grace of God go I.*

A brown bear guide who's a friend of mine once followed some tracks that led him to a kill site he found hard to believe. Don Anderson lives in Atascadero, California, works at Bear Lake Lodge during its hunting seasons, and is arguably the best professional bear hunter alive. He has seen it all, or at least he thought he had until he saw where a 9-foot-tall brown had killed and fed on an 8-foot-tall brown in the springtime snow along a frozen creek. We're talking about something the size of a Jeep attacking a Mini Cooper here, and it was no wonder half the countryside was torn up. God, I can't imagine the fight to the death that must have taken place, and it was definitely nature at its fiercest.

Don kept tracking the bigger bear and finally his client and he killed it, having read the full story of its cannibalism in the snow. It had come out of its mountainside den, lain in the sun for a couple of days, passed the hibernation waste out of its bowels, and then gone on the prowl. Every brown bear in the world does the same every spring, leastwise if they live in the colder climates, since it's stamped in their brains.

I would always marvel at them when I'd fly my airplane or helicopter just before breakup, and whether it was in Prince William Sound, on Kodiak Island, or along the Alaskan Peninsula, it was the same. Tracks. Tracks where you would least expect them, and that was on top of the snow-covered mountains. The paw marks would look like someone in bunny boots was slogging across the highest peaks and then tobogganing down the far side, only to start up another winter slope. Obviously, the browns were out of their dens, but why so early when there was almost nothing for them to eat? Even the bottomlands weren't completely thawed, so what were they doing at 3,000 and 4,000 feet? It's one of nature's mysteries, but I think I know the answer.

Wildlife experts would have everyone believe that brown bear are starving and can scarcely move when they first leave their dens, but that's false. They actually have fat left over from the previous year and are pretty much ready to go, and go they do over some of the roughest mountains in the world. The bigger males come out first, get their motors started, and then take off. They're looking for two things—food and sex, but probably not in that order (boys will be boys). The reason they stay up high is strategic...or maybe premeditated.

They patrol the mountaintops for a few days and restart their digestive systems with alder buds from the higher slopes, which is the same food that ptarmigan eat. The buds act as a laxative for their winter waste and give them some sustenance. Meanwhile, spring comes to Alaska with a burst of bluebird days, golden sunshine, and no wind. The bottomlands heat up and the warm air rises, carrying all the scents to the bears waiting above. Now they have a full picture of what's going on below them—where the first green plants are sprouting; where the sows are since they are just now coming out; where the winterkilled moose are buried in the melting snow; where the dead walrus and whales are beached, and, most important of all, where the competition is, since they're all after the same thing and it's every man for himself. The oldest boars have the advantage, since there is a real pecking order in their kingdom, and they are determined to get the biggest share of everything, girls included.

Brown bear are opportunistic, besides being natural-born meat eaters, and that explains the cannibalism Don Anderson discovered. The larger boar had smelled the smaller one, attacked from above, and killed it in a horrific fight. It had killed two birds with one stone, so to speak, because it now had its first big meal, plus gotten rid of an interloper. It's always interesting to see the dominate boars and their battle scars, and their bodies are literally covered with them, especially around the head. They look as if someone has taken a meat cleaver after them when you examine their hides or see them up close in the wilds. One bear in particular comes to mind, and he was an important celebrity.

I first saw "Diver" at Brooks Falls when my wife and I flew in for a day of sightseeing and fishing. After our mandatory lesson on bear etiquette, we walked to the main platform, which was new at the time, and joined twenty-or-so others who were gathered there. There weren't a lot of bears because the salmon run had just started, but there was still more than enough action to keep everyone interested. A half dozen browns had formed a veritable picket line and it was woe to any fish that tried making it past the falls. Clearly, we were watching a group of skilled fishermen.

One bear was a mammoth brute that weighed 1,500 pounds. You can always identify a huge boar by its gunnysack-sized head and paunchy belly that almost drags the ground, and Diver was no exception. The unusual thing about him, though, was his blond ears, which set him apart from all the others. You could spot him from a mile away and everyone in the park knew him by name, which he'd gotten from his specialized fishing skills. He stayed in the deeper water at the foot of the falls, held his head underwater, and waited for his salmon with his butt up in the air. It was quite a sight and had won him international fame, inasmuch as there are probably more Asians and Europeans visiting Brooks than Americans, and, of course, everyone wanted his picture. Funny some of them didn't ask for his autograph.

Later that day, I walked up to Lake Brooks and went fly fishing for rainbows at the headwaters of the Brooks River, which is not a long way above the falls. Four friends came along with me, but my wife stayed behind at the viewing platform to finish her photography, though she said she wouldn't be long. The fish weren't biting, but it was a gorgeous spot with water so clear you could see the bottom everywhere. I stayed near shore and was working my Nushagak Special behind some deep rocks in the hope of changing our luck, and my friends were doing the same in the middle of the river. Suddenly, one of them said something and I looked to my right. Here was Diver coming right at me and he'd gotten within 30 feet. I'll never forget his beat-up face and beady eyes, and I've never waded so fast in my life. Once again, the number one rule at Brooks is to get out of the way.

I managed to get myself half way across the river by the time Diver got to where I had been standing along the shoreline, so he didn't do much more than give me a dirty look. Why he had decided to leave the falls and walk upriver, who knows, but all the browns at Brooks meander around like they're in a shopping mall, which is, I suppose, not far from the truth. We had heard gunshots downriver and guessed some bears had gotten into something that was verboten. Two or three were teenagers and they were always testing the park rangers' patience. Kind of like humans in that respect.

Diver then took a left and snuck into the woods, which was puzzling. I stopped and turned around, only to see my wife step out only a few feet from where he'd made his detour. How both hadn't bumped into each other I'll never know, and what's amazing is my wife had no idea she'd walked right past him. The trees were so thick and the river was so noisy she simply hadn't realized he was almost within spitting distance. What a close-up picture that would have been.

Come to find out, the gunfire was the park rangers shooting rubber bullets at some bears that had gotten into two Germans' backpacks, which is a real no-no. Everyone is told in no uncertain terms that you must not leave anything lying around when you visit Brooks, but nonetheless the Germans had left their gear on the shoreline when they'd gone fishing along the river, blatantly ignoring park rules. It got them yelled at and escorted back to their room. Their visit was over.

Later on, I tried to get the park rangers to change their policy to an opposite tack—shoot at the people who are breaking the rules and yell at the bears. Without a doubt, that would be a lot more effective in resolving the ongoing problem that Brooks Camp faces each summer, but they wouldn't listen to me. I still think it's the smartest way to go.

Contrast the way brown bear behave around people at Brooks to what happened to Harley Sievenpiper of Juneau. He had gone deer hunting at Port Alexander on Baranof Island and disappeared, leaving the good Samaritans who finally found him in for a nasty surprise. It was lucky some of them didn't get killed.

After Sievenpiper had failed to show up at an appointed time and place, about a dozen searchers started combing the area where they thought he might be. Eventually, they found his rifle, glasses, cap, and gloves lying beside an open bog. It was evident that a brown bear had crept up and taken him without any warning, and he hadn't even gotten off a shot. Five searchers set off along a trail of shredded clothing and drag marks to locate his remains. They worked their way uphill through heavy spruce and hemlock until they had gone almost a mile, then suddenly found themselves face-to-face with an enraged brown. Their hail of bullets stopped its attack only a few feet away from them, leaving everyone shaken to the core. Sadly, what they would find next would shake them even more.

The bear had partly eaten and then cached Sievenpiper under a pile of forest debris. After that, it had lain on top of his disemboweled body to protect it from other bears and until it got hungry again. Upon examination, it was found the bear was a large male, fat as a pig, and perfectly healthy, leaving the state troopers and the bear experts who investigated the scene in great consternation. Finally, they couldn't explain away the human predation with the usual excuse of, "Oh, the bears are hungry because there are no berries." The truth of the matter was the bear simply did what it was born to do, nothing more and nothing less.

I'll try to explain why some browns attack people and others don't in the next two chapters, since, regrettably, the Brooks Fall's bears are the exception, not the rule.

Robinson R22 helicopter the author flew on two round trips between Arizona and Alaska.

Gold mining claim 100 miles north of Anchorage where the black bear stalked the author and his wife. The helicopter pad and walking trail are at the bottom, center left.

Baby seal waiting for its mother along the Bering Sea near Bear Lake Lodge. It's in great danger of brown bear predation.

Bull walrus along the Bering Sea. They don't spend their lives on the icepack as most people believe but often haul out ashore instead.

Dall Sheep ewes in Denali National Park that were photographed by the author's wife. *Where are their lambs?*

A wolf the author's wife photographed not far from the ewes. *Does he know anything about the lambs?*

A grizzly photographed by the author's wife. *Notice how their noses are always working overtime.*

Polar bears live all along Hudson Bay not far north of Minnesota.

THE FISH-EATERS

THE BROWN BEAR IS ACTUALLY THE EASIEST to get along with of all the North American bears, despite the attacks and predation that I described in the last chapter. Alaskans and all the tourists they shepherd around every summer often interact with them and are usually none the worse for it, and bear viewing has gotten to be a booming industry in the last frontier. Bush pilots, commercial seaplane operators, and fishing lodges fly people out every day to see them, particularly along Cook Inlet and the Katmai coast in Southwest Alaska, although Kodiak Island, Prince William Sound, and the Alaskan Panhandle have their fair shares as well. There's more than enough browns to go around and all it takes is a pocketbook full of disposable income to enjoy seeing them in their natural settings.

The reason for the brown bears' relatively peaceful nature is their abundant food supply, which features spawning salmon but also a diversity of other good things to eat because the Alaskan coastlines are so rich in clams, salad-like plants, and dead marine animals that drift ashore. Once again, browns are very opportunistic and somewhat humanlike in their ability to balance their diets with all sorts of things. They are much smarter and more resourceful than people give them credit for, although some experts suggest they are as smart as 3-year-old children. Here's a news flash for you—they're a lot smarter than that, and show me the little kid who can catch salmon by holding his head underwater as Diver did at Brooks Falls. Never underestimate the brown's ability to figure things out and prosper because of it.

Warren Johnson, whom I've mentioned before, tells about the time he spotted a 30-foot dead whale that had beached just south of Nelson Lagoon, a small Aleut village on the Bering Sea side of the Alaskan Peninsula. He circled with his plane and counted nine browns of assorted sizes wandering in and out of the huge carcass as if it were some kind of weird circus tent. "They go after the good parts first," he explained, "and eat the heart, liver, and kidneys, then work their way out. A sow with two cubs were waiting their turn up on a high bank, since she didn't want to take any needless chances until the bigger bears had eaten all they could." His observations are illustrative of how browns behave in their natural environment and how they've learned to share their good luck, albeit in an established pecking order. Believe it or not, humans have integrated into this ecological peace treaty from back to the last ice age.

It's clear to me that brown bears and humans have shared many of the same fishing holes since time immemorial, so they've gotten somewhat used to each other. Brooks Falls, McNeil River, Bear River, the Russian River, Karluk Lake on Kodiak Island, and I could go on and on throughout the length and breadth of Alaska, all show signs that early man was fishing side-by-side with the browns wherever there were spawning salmon. It's my belief that because browns are so single-minded when they are fishing and because they are so accustomed to people fishing near them throughout the ages, they've become somewhat tolerant of sharing that particular food with people. The bears at Brooks Falls have seen humans since the time they were babies, just as did the generations of bears before them and on down the line. It's bred into them, and so there's little danger in watching them catching salmon as has been proven for so many years. There's never been a bear attack at Brooks or McNeil, nor do I expect there ever will be as long as both remain as well managed as they have been in the past.

One can always bet there are lots of bears nearby during any salmon runs, and it instantly becomes necessary for people to modify their behavior in order to stay out of trouble. It never takes long for browns to figure out what whirring fishing reels mean or what's inside those coolers that fishermen are always carrying around. The pecking order I've talked about quickly comes into play and guess who's at the end of the waiting line, at least as far as the bears are concerned? There's such a thing as proxy subsistence fishing in Alaska, but rather than catching a limit of sockeye for your homebound grandparents, it could turn out to be for a half-ton brown.

Some good friends of mine found this out the hard way a few summers ago, and it was one of those deals where they could have gotten themselves killed. *Oh, but for the hair on your chinny, chin, chin.*

Dale "Red" Wagner is about as popular and well-known as they come in Anchorage, and he loves nothing better than enjoying Alaska's great outdoors. Supplementing his outstanding outdoor skills is his gourmet touch with salmon, and his canned sockeyes are the best in the world. I shamelessly eat more than my share whenever I can.

Every August, Red flies down along Cook Inlet to the Kustatan River when the silvers come in and he catches a big batch of them for his smokehouse. It's a ritual of his and he's often accompanied by his wife, Judy, and one or more of his pals from around town. It's a great place to fish and the action is usually hot.

On a clear day, Red and Judy left Lake Hood with their Cessna 180 floatplane and a longtime friend of theirs, Chuck Lastufka, followed behind with his Bellanca Scout, which was on floats as well. They landed on what's affectionately known as the "mud hole" and walked over to the Kustatan and started catching silvers left and right. Another fellow and his wife had flown in earlier, were fishing nearby, and had almost limited out. Things were looking good.

They were all scattered along the river, yet Red was still within eyeshot of the woman he'd just met. She had caught several silvers and stuffed them into a backpack, which was lying on shore beside her. He had lost sight of her husband and assumed he was upriver someplace. Then a silver smacked his line and the fight was on.

He had no more than landed the fish when he suddenly heard the woman start screaming, "Bear, bear, a bear's attacking me." He jumped up on the riverbank so he could see over some tall grass, but what he saw afterward was hard for him to believe.

A midsized brown shot out of an alder patch and pounced on the woman's backpack and ripped it open in almost the same motion. Then to his astonishment, the bear grabbed her camera first, bit it in two, and spit it out as if it were bad black licorice. Afterward, it started gulping down her silvers and eye-balling her as if to say, "How do you like these apples, lady?" Understandably, she got out of there.

Red grabbed his bear rifle and took off on the run to help her. When he got near the brown, he fired over its head and frightened it back into the alders. There wasn't much left of the poor woman's backpack, but there was nothing that could be done about it. Her husband ran back to see what was wrong and Red saw he had a pistol, so after a few minutes he walked back to where he'd been fishing. Later on, he worked his way downriver and lost sight of the unfortunate couple. All was quiet once again.

Pop, pop, pop, pop!

Red instantly knew the bear had returned, and he ran upriver again. Pistols just don't cut it when it comes to browns, and if one gets in its mind to attack, then somebody could get hurt or killed, and it most likely won't be the bear. When he reached the couple, they had chased off the bear once more, or one just like it, since there were now several in the area, but they'd had a bellyful of the Kustatan and were pulling out. They packed up their stuff and headed for the mud hole, where their seaplane was tied down as well. Off they went with a mighty roar.

Red, Judy, and Chuck stayed near each other and limited out as fast as they could, then set off for the mud hole as well. Judy led the way with a bag of fish, but she quickly put on the brakes when she got in sight of their two floatplanes. "Chuck, Chuck, there's a bear in your airplane and it's tearing it apart." Needless to say this was not good news, and once again Red ran forward with his rifle.

When the bear heard him coming, it crawled back out of the hole it had ripped in the side of the fabric-covered Scout, crossed over to the far side of the fuselage, stood up with its front feet on top of the airframe, and stared at him. He let drive with two blasts over its head that scared it back into the brush. All three then walked up to the airplane and looked at the damage. The backseat had been ripped out and was lying in the water, there was a flag-sized piece of fabric hanging down from the bottom of one wing, and, of course, there was the gaping hole in the fuselage. Chuck was sick. He had just bought the airplane and paid a lot of money for it.

"What am I going to do? My airplane is so wrecked I don't know if it's even safe to fly."

Red kept his head on a swivel, since he knew there was more than one bear close by.

"Well, it'll be nothing but a scrap pile by tomorrow morning if you leave it here. You've got to fly it, and I'll stay alongside you and keep an eye on things."

Just then he saw a brown coming at them through the brush, and it was getting really close. He fired directly at it, even though he couldn't get a clear shot. It dodged back into the bushes and disappeared. *Now what?* he wondered.

He snuck over and searched for blood and hair but couldn't find any. Meanwhile, he glimpsed another bear or maybe the same one. Regardless, it was time to help Chuck get ready to go. They were nothing but mouth-watering bait with all their fish and an airplane that a bear didn't want to leave alone. Clearly, it would keep coming back, and there was no sense in tempting fate, especially since he was now running low on ammunition.

Chuck did a masterful job of milking his Scout back into Anchorage, and all three came away with an unforgettable experience. I'll always remember when I drove past his plane at Lake Hood and saw the damage. I hadn't seen an airplane get beaten up by a bear before, and the damage was amazing. People forget that bush pilots often fly into isolated places with their $100,000 or $200,000 airplanes and suddenly find their lives on the line. Chuck could have just as well crashed and burned.

The big problem with the Kustatan bears is they've learned what all those noisy seaplanes mean, and it has gotten a little like how African loins and hyenas behave when they see circling vultures. They instantly know there's an easy meal to be had and come on the run. The Kustatan browns have gotten bolder as the years have passed and become more persistent in their quest to steal from the fishermen they find along the river. It all leads to people-bear conflicts where one or the other ends up half scared to death, injured, or dead. A small brown was killed and left to rot on a sandbar in the summer of 2007. Alaska has faced ever-increasing problems like this with its brown bear population and, sadly, there's no easy solution. The state's human population is growing and there's no shortage of bears, and so it's to be expected the two parties will find themselves eyeball to eyeball at the best fishing spots. Oddly, I'm reminded of the movie, *Cool Hand Luke,* where the salient line was, "What we've got here is failure to communicate."

The bottom line is the bears are being baited, intentionally or unintentionally, and it's been going on for a long time. Fishermen fly into the Kustatan or a river just like it, catch salmon like crazy, fillet them and leave the heads, guts, and eggs scattered around, so it's inevitable the bears smell this and start feeding on the leftovers. It never takes long for them to figure out, "Hey, why in hell don't I just speed up this whole process and steal the fish, since I'm easily five times bigger than the stupid-looking creature that's catching them." The bear has no way of knowing the fisherman intends on using lethal force to protect himself or herself, mostly because he or she has heard countless stories about Alaskan bears attacking people. Bang, bang, and the bear is dead, although in some cases it's the fisherman who gets the worst of it.

Daniel Bigley, who at the time lived 40 miles east of Anchorage in the small settlement of Girdwood, stands out as a prime example of how badly things can go wrong when bears and people gather at a place where there's been salmon carcasses strewn six ways to Sunday. He paid an extreme price for the laisser-faire attitude of the U.S. Forest Service, the U.S. Fish and Wildlife Service, and the State of Alaska for letting this carelessness reach a crisis point. It wasn't like the whole world didn't know there was a dangerous problem, but, as usual, it turned out to be the old story of closing the barn door after the horses had run off.

Alaskans joke about combat fishing and there's no better example of this than when the spawning sockeyes hit the confluence of the Kenai and Russian Rivers every June and July. Thousands of anglers from Anchorage and the Kenai Peninsula overrun this age-old hotspot, its parking lots and campgrounds, and everyplace in between as folks shoulder their way into the infinite lines of fishermen who are intent on catching their limits of the best tasting salmon known to God. It's a madhouse of tangled fishing lines, folks getting slapped upside the head with fishing rods, and F-bombs because someone just got snagged by a barbed hook. Then to add to the melee are the ubiquitous backpacks, coolers, and fish guts that forever go along with a setting like this. Is it any wonder the area's brown bears want to join in on all the fun, but it's turned the Russian into a powder keg, particularly since about a million people are packing six guns? It should be no surprise to anyone that this isn't one of Alaska's better wilderness experiences.

In the summer of 2003, Dan drove to the Russian River with his dog and a friend and spent the day fishing, or should I say fighting, for what Alaskans like to call reds. They quit at suppertime, ate at a nearby restaurant, and then hit the river again for some nighttime angling when there are lots less people getting in the way. After catching their limits, they headed for their car but never made it. A sow brown flattened Dan and savaged him unmercifully, with the greatest damage being done to his head. His forehead, eyes, and nose, for all practical purposes, were turned to mush, and then for good measure the rest of his body was badly mauled as well. The sow had gotten his facial bones in her teeth and all but pulverized them, and there was little hope he would live.

Against all odds, a mercy flight by helicopter and the miracle work of a young surgeon saved Dan's life. After a short hiatus, he returned to Alaska, married, had a baby boy, and put his life together again despite being a blinded, disfigured, and facing the trauma of losing so much of his earlier independence as an outdoor adventurer. He's working with special children and once again taking on the world with his indomitable spirit. I wish him all the best.

I stopped at the Russian River and snooped around right after he'd been mauled, and, understandably, everyone I talked to was really jumpy. Let's just say it would have been a bad time to show up in a gorilla outfit or start growling and jumping out of the bushes to scare your friends. The bear that had attacked him had hit and run and was no where to be found, and there were differing stories as to what had happened. Nighttime fishing had been banned and state and federal workers had gotten tough on people and their careless habits with their food, fish, and garbage. As expected, the official line was the bear had been protecting her cubs, but that left lots of questions unanswered, at least in my mind. Supposedly, the cubs had been big enough to take care of themselves.

I came away with my mind made up that it was the classic situation of Dan and his friend not having been sufficiently aware of their surroundings, ala Daniel Boone style. It was no secret there were aggressive bears around, but both young men were feeling good about themselves, no doubt chatting up a storm about the great time they'd had, and simply weren't being cautious enough. It was much too late by the time they saw the bear. Nevertheless, the thing that puzzled me the most, and still does to this day, is the dog missed warning them in time, which is really unusual. Dogs almost always sense bears from a long way off, but this one didn't, and all I can think of is it was caught up in Dan and his friend's enthusiasm over their successful trip, was dancing around and not paying attention, and got caught off guard.

My checking into the mauling gives me the opportunity to put forward something I've observed through the years, and that's the timeworn excuse of, "Oh, the sow was only protecting her cubs," is seldom the *true* reason behind such an attack and simply illustrates the general lack of knowledge about bears. Most often the attacks by brown bear sows that are with their cubs represent a situation where the cubs aren't that much smaller than their mothers, and so what on earth are they being protected from? They can fend for themselves, especially against any scrawny human who would be dumb enough to mess with them, and it's my belief the sows know this or they wouldn't behave in quite the way they do. *And so what gives?* Certainly, Dan, his friend, and his dog weren't doing anything that could have been perceived as threatening. Hell, they didn't even know she and her cubs were there. My mind has been made up for a long time it all has to do with sows teaching their cubs to be masters of their own destinies. The old shoot first and ask questions later approach, if you get what I mean.

All the world's big predators teach their young to show unbridled aggression, kill or be killed, and that predation is a fundamental source of food. Ain't pretty, but that's the way Mother Nature works, so don't eat sausage if you don't like watching how it's made. Nowadays you can hardly turn on the television without seeing a cheetah carrying back a half-alive gazelle for her cubs to kill or much the same thing as a tiger mother emasculates her prey and then let's junior finish the job with a choke hold. Ugly, ugly, but don't get me wrong—you can go all the way back to the dinosaurs and the natural world hasn't changed, nor should it. It's the survival of the fittest and how every species on this earth keeps up with the laws of evolution. Don't expect mother bears to leave their babies stuck on stupid.

Look at it this way, brown bear sows *run away* if their main concern is protecting their cubs. Who's going to catch them? Certainly no humans and damn few other wild creatures as well. As I've said before, you're talking about animals that can hit an uptown speed limit in the blink of an eye. I'm convinced that most attacks on humans by brown bear sows are overt acts, showing their cubs the basics of bear communications, or in much pithier terms, how to talk bear to people so they don't forget.

But what they're *really* doing is teaching by example, and this is best seen when a sow comes down to a river where there's spawning salmon. There are always other bears around and they're usually lots bigger than she is, but that doesn't stop her from fishing. She carefully approaches the shoreline with her cubs right behind her and then strategically positions them on the riverbank with her facial expressions, posturing, and throaty sounds. They stay put and intently watch her, and then she starts fishing. Another bear, usually a boar twice her size, sooner or later gets a little too close to the invisible perimeter she's set up. Instantly, she goes absolutely postal and flies into a maniacal, foaming-at-the-mouth rage. She slaps him around and makes him back up with a display of ferocity that would make a bull elephant crap in his pants. You can almost see it on the boar's face, "Jesus Christ, lady, all I was doing was minding my own business and I hardly looked at your cubs, so give me a break." Be that as it may, that particular bear and every other one around have suddenly gotten the message. *"Don't mess with me or I'll turn you into hamburger!"*

Meanwhile, her cubs are watching all this and saying, *"Wow, look at you, mom. You're wonderful!"* But the real lesson is the positive reinforcement of how they feel about her and, more importantly, how they should react when threatened by anything or anyone. They've just learned ferocity often trumps size and how dominance is established in their species. In order for them to survive she must act as a positive role model, though the sad part is sometimes humans get in the way of this phenomenon and suffer accordingly.

At any rate, baiting, however it occurs, is a constant problem and always leads to conflicts where either a bear ends up dead or someone gets hurt or killed. I'll never forget the time I got crosswise of two fishermen along the Upper Copper River during its annual dip netting extravaganza, and I'm not using the word extravaganza lightly, since it's something to see. Subsistence fishermen from all over Central Alaska flock to the old gold rush settlement of Chitina (actually copper is what made the town), four-wheel an abandoned railroad bed south into the Wood Canyon, and then hang onto its rock faces for dear life while dipping long-handled fishnets into eddying depths the color of coffee and cream. You haven't a prayer if you fall in, so this adventure is a lot better suited to the *clavadistas* (cliff divers) of La Quebrada, Mexico, than ordinary fishermen, and a good many folks have drowned in the fast-moving waters the graybeards like to describe as too thick to drink and too thin to plow. It's definitely not a place for the fainthearted or those who are afraid of heights.

I had ridden into the canyon as far as a waterfall called Haley Creek and was trying to find an old, secret footpath leading up into the Chugach Mountains. I finally figured it out and discovered that if you walked through a railroad tunnel that had been blasted through a steep mountain in 1908, took a fishhook turn at its far end, and climbed on top of the tunnel you could still find traces of this hidden trail. The problem was, though, an excellent argument could be made that Mount McKinley might be easier to climb because the mountainside was so choked with alders. I gave it up and decided there wasn't any way I could make that climb with a fifty or sixty pound pack, not to mention there wasn't any drinking water handily available. Maybe if I was twenty years old and hired some Sherpas...anyway, you get the picture.

It was getting late by the time I got back down to Haley Creek, and so I decided to camp overnight among the fishermen who were gathered there. There's a sandy place near where Haley dumps into the river and folks pitch their tents, build campfires, and get ready for the next day of death-wish dipnetting. Of course, one of the things you must do to sufficiently prepare yourself is to knock back some six packs of beer. It was just my luck to run into two guys who were over their quotas and were tossing fish scraps along the shoreline so they could watch a couple of small brown bear come get them. Other campers were coming up and taking pictures, and there was a bit of a commotion going on with the predictable contest of who could get the closest to these small browns that were just getting out on their own. I didn't like what I was seeing and said so, pointing out that among other things there were little kids in camp and sooner or later those two teenage browns would tear into somebody's tent. Besides, I said, there was a state wildlife trooper who patrolled the area and he would likely slap them with a fine if he caught them baiting bears. Unfortunately, my preaching didn't go over too well, though they did stop what they were doing. But this is a perfect example of how so many people/bear conflicts get started in the first place and why one side or the other ends up dead.

The rest of the story, as Paul Harvey would say, is the absolute fascination in bears that has now spread worldwide, which for better or worse, has placed Alaska's brown bears dead center in the crosshairs. The last frontier not only has the world's largest population of them, but it's also the home of the biggest ones. Although it would be an extraordinary specimen, it's quite likely that one weighing more than a ton could be found on Kodiak Island, somewhere along the Alaskan Peninsula, or on Unimak Island, which is the start of the Aleutian Chain. The rest of the world's brown bear run only half as big and there's not nearly as many. Understandably, everyone wants to see the monsters of the midnight sun.

With that in mind, Haley Creek was inconsequential as compared to what's happening today, with bear viewing and bear photography taking on the proportions of the 1897 Klondike Gold Rush. ...On second thought, my analogy is pretty bad— one hundred thousand people set out for Alaska back then and less than a third made it, but now there are almost two million visiting the state each year. Needless to say, the pressure is on.

I had written in the first chapter that bear viewing has grown into a booming business and reached a size that worries me. In 1972, I started selling Cessna and Piper floatplanes to Alaskan bush pilots who primarily used them for personal transportation, although some went to big-game hunting guides and small air-taxi operators. My sales increased dramatically through the years until my company, St. Cloud Aviation, Inc. of St. Cloud, Minnesota, had won Cessna Aircraft Company's single-engine sales awards for 1979 and 1980. My sales manager and I sold 40 brand-new Cessna 206 floatplanes in one year alone, let alone innumerable other models, with almost all of them heading north. I set up a branch operation on Lake Hood in Anchorage in 1983, which, once again, is the largest seaplane base in the world, and I sold more floatplanes, but now they were getting bigger. The deHavilland Beavers and Otters were becoming popular, despite both models being 30 years old. The air-taxi operators were no longer small-sized and now everyone was getting into the fishing lodge business, and these time-honored planes could carry twice as many passengers. By 1990, lots of Alaskans were learning there was extra money to be made by flying tourists out to see bears along the salmon streams. Suddenly, the race was on.

Once, where there was only a half-dozen businesses that were flying people out to see bears, now there's probably a hundred or more—and that doesn't take into account the numerous tourist operators who use boats to do the same thing. The poor bears scarcely have any time alone any more, and it's gotten almost like bleacher seats along some of the salmon streams where the audience cheers when one catches a fish (people actually clap and cheer at Brooks Falls). What's next—cheerleaders dressed like the Dallas Cowgirls dancing along the shorelines, leading the people in their applause? I realize I'm being pretty facetious, but I want to make my point. The very wilderness experience that everyone so dearly wants is being overrun by too damn many people. But what's *really* important is what's happening to the bears, and it can't be good. They're under enough stress as it is.

Brown bears are solitary animals by habit, except large numbers of them will often come together when a food source is located at a specific place, as I've said before. But you don't have to watch them long before you realize there's lots of animosity between them as they sort out who's top dog and on down the line. Sometimes, terrible fights break out, particularly between the boars, and the hunks of flesh they tear out of each other can be as big as beef steaks. *Talk about tension in the air*—then you add a bunch of tourists to make things even worse. Click up bear viewing on the Internet and take a close look at the pictures, or watch for the same thing on television when you can. Without fail, you will see the bears glancing back or looking sideways at the cameras and asking themselves, "What in hell is this all about?" Carnival-like bear viewing has added a new wrinkle to their lives and they don't know quite what to think about it. I'm not sure it's all that healthy for the brown bear population over the long run, at least if it goes unchecked as the new millennium rolls by, and there must be some level at which we reach a breaking point.

This leads me to believe that most brown bear attacks such as Dan Bigley's are more about, "I'm mad as hell and I'm not going to take it anymore," than anything else, and it's about anger management on the bear's part, if you will. Look at it this way—*what if there were people watching you with binoculars or taking pictures of you no matter what you did?* Doesn't make any difference whether you're taking a pee, breastfeeding your kids, or trying to sleep—they're watching, watching, and watching. How long do think it would take you before you'd flip *your* lid? That's more or less what's happening with lots of brown bear nowadays.

Wait a minute, you say, they're just dumb animals and don't even know the difference, and it's not like they're people. But that's where humans have it wrong—bears are a lot like people, and you don't have to study them long before you realize there are key similarities. There are big ones and little ones, grumpy ones and friendly ones, most are patient but some are hot-tempered, and every imaginable thing in between. They are creatures of habit, naturally curious, treasure their privacy, and hold grudges forevermore. I'll grant you that it's on a different kind of playing field, now that humans have left the Stone Age, gone plastic, and landed on the moon, but it's still wrong to assume we're godlike creatures who don't have to pay a price if we keep snooping where we don't belong.

The McNeil River Sanctuary probably exemplifies the best in brown bear viewing, even from *their* point of view. It's micromanaged by the State of Alaska, done on a lottery system as I've said before, and once you've slogged in hip boots the two miles or so it takes to get there, you are restricted to a small gravel patch. Armed Fish and Game employees escort you there and back, and if you decide that you must cut your day short and return to camp for whatever reason, everyone must leave right along with you. Everything is highly regimented, low impact, and done in a way that pretty much leaves all the animals that live around there in an acceptable wild state. Seals, foxes, wolves, and whatever else that likes fresh salmon are often seen in the area as well.

The flip side of McNeil is something called the "Bear Farm," which is actually a summer place owned by a retired Anchorage schoolteacher named Charles Vandergaw. He made celebrity status in 2007 after the *Anchorage Daily News*, along with assorted other newspapers and websites, featured photographs of him communing with the black and the brown bears that hang around his cabin for the free handouts he gives them every day. A British filmmaker even filmed a documentary titled, *The Man who lives with Bears,* which highlighted his supposed supernatural gift of being a "bear whisperer." Just so you know where I'm going with all this, anyone can become a bear whisperer if you fly in dog food by the ton and start feeding them, but it doesn't make you particularly smart, or for that matter, truly caring of a unique wildlife species. But as with most things in life, the story is far more complicated than with what one sees at first glance.

I've known bits and pieces about Charlie and his bear farm for a long time, since it's almost impossible to keep a secret like that from a place like Lake Hood. His neighbors and he can't access their summer cabins without using floatplanes, and that was my business for over thirty years, besides selling all kinds of parts and repairs to keep those airplanes in the air. Keeping something like that from the thousands of bush pilots who fly in the Anchorage area is something like the silly old joke about Alaskan wives never worry about their husbands cheating on them, since they can see them all summer and track them all winter. Furthermore, Charlie's place isn't that far off the flight path I would take between Lake Hood and the gold claim that my wife and I own, and it's awfully hard not to go snooping when you fly your own helicopter. Nonetheless, I must admit I had no idea of the extent of his "playing with bears," which, if you remember, I criticized early in this book.

Charlie has gotten himself, a dozen or more bears, his surrounding neighbors, and the Alaska Department of Fish and Game into a giant pickle, especially since not long ago that very organization sanctioned a liberalized bear hunt in the same area, allowing, among other things, flying and shooting on the same day and unlimited kills, even of sows and cubs. Clearly, it's become one of those Catch-22 situations that makes you want to scream, "Stop the world and let me off!" None of it makes any sense, especially since the least that will likely happen is several bears will end up dead just because of the very things that have been done by the guy who says he loves them.

Look at it this way. Charlie isn't a young man, and so it's only a matter of time before he'll have to stop flying, or on the worst case basis, the grim reaper will suddenly decide it's time for him to join the great bear whisperer in the sky. *Now what?* Do you really think someone else will want to go out to his cabin and try living with a bunch of freeloading bears, at least one of which has a hair-trigger temper? —while Charlie was letting the Brits film him and his furry friends, a female brown tore the hell out of one his hands, resulting in a quick trip to an emergency room in Anchorage. Somehow I keep hearing a realtor asking in the future, "Is that with or without the bears?" And then there's the requirement that you should list all the discrepancies of the real estate you wish to sell. That ought to be interesting.

The underlying problem is the Arkansas-sized area that lies northwest of Anchorage is perfect moose habitat, except there's very few moose. It's rough, strewn with small lakes and bottomless bogs, thick forests and deep rivers, and there's a big lack of roads. Meantime, there are lots of folks living on remote homesteads who are raising kids and sled dogs, and so they go hungry if they don't harvest a moose. The pressure is on the politicians to do something about it, with lots of their constituents being Native Alaskans who were guaranteed subsistence hunting rights long ago by both the federal and state governments. Understandably, the word has been passed down to get rid of the bears, of which it's been discovered have gotten exceptionally skilled at killing most of the moose calves every spring. Of course, all the wildlife organizations don't agree that's actually happening, but that only makes it much easier for you to understand how Charlie fits into this mind-boggling conundrum. He's on a lot of people's shit list and Lord knows how it all will work out, especially since, short of the state hiring a helicopter gunship, there's no way to kill very many bears anyway. The country is simply so wild and swampy there's little incentive for anyone to hunt them for any reason.

But here's the big picture—Alaska's brown bears are coming under increasing pressure that's causing them to lose their wild state, or maybe I should say their fear of man. People are buying million dollar airplanes to haul tourists out by the truck load to see them, so there's the inevitable pushing and shoving between the bear-viewing businesses to outdo each other. They must make their bank payments and meet their payrolls, and the only way to do that is to offer a better product. Who can get the closest, see the most bears, and that sort of thing.

How long do you suppose it will take, if it's not happening already, for those folks who are falling behind financially to ask themselves, "Hmmm, dog food, why didn't I think of that?" And so it goes. Even the National Park Service is a participant in this rising crosswind of storm clouds. Their budget is based on visitors, and what park manager doesn't want more visitors so he or she can hire more employees to boss around, because, let's face it, it's all about money. Lots of money.

The dirty little secret that almost no one knows about is the National Park Service does its headcounts in both directions, or better said, pencil whips the numbers. For example, if Lake Clark National Park (another brown bear hotspot) has a thousand visitors fly in, they record it as two thousand because they must fly back out. Again, it's all about the money, except it's the bears that are paying the price. And there can be no better explanation for what was behind Timothy Treadwell and Amy Huguenard's horrific deaths. Mr. Vicious had had enough…but you must remember it cost him his life, right along with one of his little buddies.

 # SNEAK ATTACKS

THE MOST MYSTERIOUS ALASKAN BROWN BEAR attack in recent
times took place on May 25, 1999, on the Kenai Peninsula not
far from the small town of Soldotna. A longtime friend of mine,
Ron Davis, who I went to high school with in Minnesota, lives
there, along with Ted Spraker, a wildlife biologist who worked
twenty-eight years for the Alaska Department of Fish and Game.
Both know a lot about bears, inasmuch as Ron has flown for
more than forty years in the Alaskan bush and among his many
accomplishments is he always flies the world famous Iditarod
Sled Dog Trail with his Cessna 185 ski-plane for the Iron Dog
snowmobile race, which runs almost twice the distance of the
dogs. That takes him across some of the world's most forbidding
mountains and wilderness areas in early February, the worst
part of winter, and so the only criticism I've ever had for him
is he likes to study his brown bears from about 5,000 feet, and
the altitude tends to get a little higher as he grows older. Ted's
expertise speaks for itself, plus he was the fellow assigned the
responsibility for investigating one of the greatest riddles of all
bear attacks, and interestingly, not far from where Ron and he

live. Ted and I know some of the same people because the State of Alaska has bought airplanes and helicopters from me and our paths have crossed before.

Ken Cates was a 53-year-old building-trades supervisor who loved the Alaskan outdoors and spent as much time as he could hunting, fishing, or just taking long hikes on secluded trails. He liked attending church and helping needy neighbors, yet preferred his own company and keeping his thoughts to himself. The construction industry on the Kenai Peninsula and in Anchorage knew him well for his professional skills and being an all-around good guy. His wife, Sharon, and he had just decided to wind it down, build a retirement home, and take life easy.

At lunchtime, he told Sharon that he was taking off for the Funny River Trail for one of his usual jaunts, and she answered she was going shopping. He grabbed his daypack, a lightweight camp stove, some dried soup, and a Winchester bolt-action rifle. The Funny River is an old horse trail that runs a long way south of Soldotna through a big wilderness area toward the Kenai Mountains and the Harding Ice Field. It starts out flat and boggy-like with plenty of trees but then rises as you go along, and, of course, it's full of animals because it runs through a wildlife refuge. That's the one thing that's nice about the Kenai Peninsula, since the wilderness lies right out your backdoor.

Back at home, Sharon began to worry in the late afternoon because Ken hadn't returned, and then at suppertime she couldn't stand it anymore and telephoned a friend. They drove to the Funny River trailhead and found his pickup parked alongside the road, but no sign of him. Now she was scared to death and not long afterward called the state troopers. They reassured her that the Kenai Refuge was nothing but a spidery labyrinth and he had most likely gotten himself lost but would come back soon with nothing more than sore feet. She wasn't so sure and started calling his friends to come look for him. Early the next morning, more than three dozen of them headed into the woods, intent on finding him on a gloomy, drizzly day. Almost immediately, some of them found his boot tracks on a narrow, muddy footpath, but much to their alarm, the paw marks of a brown bear as well, looking every bit as if it was tracking him like a bloodhound. Everyone went on high alert.

Two miles up the trail they found Ken's body lying face up on a right-hand corner, with the macabre scene initially seeming so bizarre it even fooled a state trooper into thinking he was looking at a suicide. Ken's rifle, along with an ejected shell, was lying on the ground and his little stove and a pot of water were sitting undisturbed alongside a log, but nothing else looked particularly out of place...except for the oddity of Ken's head looking as if it had been partly blown off from a self-inflicted gunshot wound. An official investigation began, which is where Ted Spraker came in.

A bit earlier, the searchers had found where the bear had left the trail and cut into the woods, along with having stopped and torn up some tundra in one spot. Why it had done that, no one knows, but it was quickly evident the brown had attacked Ken from behind, bit into his shoulder and then on the head so viciously that it had crushed his skull and killed him instantly. At some moment before his death, Ken had seen the bear and fired twice, since there was an empty round on the ground and another still in the barrel. Everything seemed to translate into he'd only had four or five seconds to save himself.

Further investigation found blood and hair on the ground and smeared on a nearby tree, as if the bear had lain down, bled a little, and then brushed against some rough bark as it had gotten back up to leave. Ken had hit the bear at least once, maybe twice, but not hard enough to do any mortal damage, since it was clear the man-killer had simply walked, if not ran away. Unluckily, the rainy day persisted, which made a detailed investigation almost impossible, since all the evidence was being washed away faster than it could be found. Consequently, Ted was forced to write a report with little in the way of hard evidence, leaving him to speculate on many aspects of what had led up to Ken's death.

It appeared the camp stove might have been the biggest culprit, since it was one of those that sounds like a big blowtorch when you turn it on. Every outdoorsman does it—you light the burner, set the water pot in place, and then sit there waiting for it to boil so you can stir in your dried soup. It's all rather mesmerizing and I've often done it myself. You're hungry, happy, and not paying any attention to your surroundings.

Ken never heard the bear until it was too late. He grabbed his rifle, turned, snapped off a shot at pointblank range, jacked in another round, but that one went straight up in the air as the bear grabbed him.

There's no question in my mind he hit the bear with the initial round, but two things went wrong. He wasn't carrying a big enough rifle and there's not much to shoot at when a brown flies at you head-on, particularly when you're in an awkward position. Ted remembered the caliber as something like a .260 and I was told by someone else it had been a .280, but in either case those are deer-sized rounds, not brown bear bullets (actually, though it's of little importance, as a Winchester bolt-action it probably would have had to have been either a .264 or a 270). Regardless, it was like bringing a knife to a gunfight, particularly with what Ted discovered in his following investigation.

He measured the bear's front paw width at 8½ inches. *That's huge!* I have a record-class brown that I shot at Bear Lake many years ago, and it's what hunters call a 10½ or 11-foot brown, which has to do with the math of squaring the hide after the bear has been skinned in preparation for a full-sized mount. My bear's front paws only measure 8 inches wide. Now maybe the mud Ted had to work with was squished out a little so his measurement could have been a bit off, but in any event the brown that killed Ken Cates was an old boar of enormous size. You're not going to kill a bear like that with a deer rifle when he's coming headlong at you, not unless you're lucky enough to hit him right between the eyes and the bullet penetrates the brain. Otherwise, you won't even knock him down, and all you've done is make him madder. *Lots madder.*

Ted thought that Ken may have seen the bear stalking him and fired over its head with the first round, which then triggered the attack. I can be easily convinced of that, but it doesn't really change anything. Clearly, the bear charged at some point and Ken tried defending himself with the only thing he had, which was too little, too late. An additional thing Ted talked about, which is something I've constantly preached about in this book, was the critical importance of staying keenly aware of your environment and the things that are going on around you. As a result, he reminded me of something that I have forgotten to talk about, and that's everyone's little forest friends. The birds and the squirrels will always tell you who else is in the woods if you know how to watch them and listen to what they're saying. I'll bet you almost anything there were ravens, magpies, and Gray Jays watching the whole savage attack unfold, since they never miss a trick, or maybe I should say a large predator. Following bears so they can pick up the scraps is one of the ways they make their living.

A full-scale search was launched for the wounded bear, but to no avail. It was long gone or had crawled into a foxhole somewhere, because despite people hunting for it from the air and on the ground, no brown of that size was ever seen again. I'm not surprised, because once an old boar like that takes off it may be several miles before he decides to slow down again. It was a sad end to an awful tragedy, but maybe some good will come of it. Never stop looking around and listening in brown bear country or get yourself into a vulnerable position. I'm sure that bear had been shot and wounded before, hated humans, had just come out of its den and was hungry, with its teeth and bones hurting because of its advanced age. It stalked Ken because it saw him as an easy target, except it didn't quite work out that way. Ken almost got him.

With that in mind, it should be pointed out there has always been an ongoing dispute in Alaska about what's the best bear gun to stop an attack, particularly as it concerns brown bears. Most arguments are centered around calibers such as the .338 and .375, both of which have been around a long time and for all practical purposes are more or less equal. With rare exceptions, almost all Alaskan bear guides carry one or the other, and both cartridges have proven themselves countless times on dangerous game, even in Africa. However, the thing that's *not* well known is most browns are killed by two people, with both using magnum rifles of one sort or another. It all has to do with hunting regulations, safety practices, and the humane killing of dangerous animals. I bring this up so everyone can better understand what people face when they venture onto the Alaskan Peninsula, Kodiak Island, or any other place that has a substantial population of SUV-sized bears. It's not so easy to kill one of them, regardless of your firearm.

Professional bear guides always tell their hunting clients in no uncertain terms to aim carefully at the bear's front shoulder and break it down, which usually stops the bear from getting up again because it's been hit in a vital area. The second thing they stress is the hunter is never to stop shooting until he or she has been told to do so. Once the guides feel those instructions have sunk in, they will begin the stalk, but then what surprises most clients is how close the guides will sneak up on a bear without it knowing. Fifty yards or less is preferable to assure an instant kill. Not until then is the hunter signaled to start firing. But what the hunter *isn't* told is if that bear doesn't immediately go down or so much as wiggles as if it might get up again, the guide will start firing with his own rifle. They aren't going to take any chances, and why should they when you think about it, especially if you feel any revulsion for what happened to Ken Cates. Only one of two things will happen—an enraged brown bear will come after them when their rifles are almost empty or dive into the alders and wait to even the score later. Neither is a desirable situation, as you can well imagine. Ergo, most brown bears are killed by a hail of bullets, usually from the professional guides (yes, most hunting clients can't hit a city bus).

The point in telling you all this is so the complexities of choosing a "bear gun" is better understood as it applies to stopping a brown bear attack. You might as well go into the field with nothing unless the particular firearm you've chosen has the right ballistics, which means tremendous knockdown power, *plus* you need to be a practiced marksman who can snap off a shot and hit something the size of a coffee cup at close range. Otherwise, you may very well be better off using bear spray or letting the bear take you down and zapping it with a stun gun or stabbing it with your knife. Making a bad shot with an inadequate weapon and wounding a brown bear will almost always exacerbate the situation, which means you will surely end up dead. Brown bears are massive animals, powerfully built, and can withstand fatal wounds with hardly a flinch. There are countless stories of them being shot right through the heart and lungs and running into heavy cover or even swimming lakes as if they'd never been hit. When their adrenaline gets pumping, it takes an extraordinary weapon to flatten them, especially if they're coming at you head-on. Be forewarned that deer rifles just aren't going to do it.

When I first moved to Alaska, one of my favorite people was a scruffy-looking hunting guide named Dana Patterson who always had an infectious grin on his face. Sadly, he died in an airplane crash some years after I'd first met him, which unfortunately happens to way too many people who make their living by hunting and fishing in the great frontier. He always booked a few clients who wanted to hunt brown bear and usually guided in the Iliamna Lake area, which is one of the largest lakes in North America. It's a wonderful place that's the headwaters of all the greatest salmon spawns in the world, and so it always has lots of brown bears running around.

One day, Dana and I were visiting about bear hunting in my office and somewhere in the conversation I asked him what he used when he was out with one of his hunters and stalking a big bear. I'll never forget what he told me. "I got a sawed-off .458," he answered, "because when I go into the brush after a wounded one I want to knock it flat even if I only hit it in the toenail."

For those who don't know about the .458 Winchester Magnum, it's the bolt-action rifle that changed the whole world of African safari hunting in 1956, since it pretty much relegated the old British double-barreled express rifles to the trash bin. It's a true elephant gun and you still see them in use when you're watching game reserve managers on television in such places as South Africa or Zambia. It's the ultimate big-game gun and clearly has the ballistics it takes to stop an attack by a man-killer right in its tracks, even if you miss by a little. No doubt that particular caliber is a bit of overkill when it comes to brown bears, but it's making the mistake in the right direction. Most times, I see people carrying pistols and 12-gauge shotguns as bear guns and they're simply not powerful enough to put down a 1,200-pound brown with any degree of certainty when one's coming at you full tilt. It's been proven in ballistics' testing that a 12-guage shotgun slug won't even penetrate a brown bear's skull unless it's within 15 yards, and to make matters worse, almost none of the various models have decent enough sights so you can make an accurate shot anyway. I think it's better to leave the duck guns at home and go for the heavy artillery or don't carry anything at all.

I wrote earlier about faithfully carrying my 30-06 Remington semiautomatic carbine when I'm in bear country, but I've always thought that gun was the *minimum* it would take to knock down a big brown, and that was only because it has a ten-shot clip and I'm a good shot, even on running targets. There's plenty of magnum calibers that are much better rifles, but the problem with them is they almost always come as bolt-actions, which means you must aim, fire, then take them off your shoulder and jack in another round. That takes way too much time if you're in a tight spot like Ken Cates found himself and the bear will usually get you before you get him. With my 30-06, all I have to do is hold point and start pulling the trigger. It's all about firepower in my humble opinion.

Actually, I could never make myself spend the money but it occurred to me long ago the *best* bear gun in the world would be the Browning .338 Winchester Magnum semiautomatic rifle that had been modified by a good gunsmith into a lightweight carbine with a ten-shot clip. It would cost big bucks to get one built, but I can't think of a more lethal weapon if you had a buffalo-sized bear coming at you from just a few feet. At any rate, everyone's selection of the right bear gun needs to be well thought out according to his or her individual needs.

I think one of the most misunderstood things about brown bears is their feisty courage and their doggedness in standing their ground once they decide something belongs to them. I have a story to illustrate what I mean.

For years, I had heard rumors about the brown bears on Kodiak Island and the Alaskan Peninsula that would stand and try picking a fight with the Alaska Department of Fish and Game helicopters that were maneuvering at close quarters to dart them for research purposes. Fish and Game often works in the field to examine the health, size, and populations of its different bear species and nothing works better than something like the Bell JetRanger. That's a good-sized ship that sounds something like a full-blown hurricane when it's hovering overhead, so I was always curious as whether or not this might be true, but I was never able to find anyone who had witnessed it.

Twice, my wife and I flew our Robinson R22 helicopter on round trips between Phoenix, Arizona, and Anchorage, Alaska, which is maybe more adventure than anyone deserves in his or her lifetime. It's 4,000 miles each way and takes you over some of the wildest parts of the world. The toughest part of the trip is always the cross-country leg between Fort Nelson, British Columbia, and Watson Lake in the Yukon Territory, which takes you down the last part of the Toad River and then over such fun places as Hell's Gate, the Rapids of the Drowned, and Boiler Canyon on the fearsome Liard River. This is a Class V white-water river that whipsaws its way through the northern end of the Rocky Mountains, then off into the Yukon wild, and it has never failed to make my hair stand on end whenever I'm flying it. Then you throw in some bad weather and high winds to make things lots more exciting and you have yourself a true circus ride. Once a friend asked me what I'd do if my engine ever failed over this butt-puckering stretch and I simply answered, "Roll my helicopter over and kill myself as fast as possible." There's never much room for an emergency landing no matter what altitude you use.

On one particular flight the weather wasn't a factor, since it was an electric-blue day without a breath of wind. It was one of those few times where you can sit back and relax as a pilot and watch for wildlife. I looked it up in my logbook and it was on April 14, 1997, and so the mountains and bottomlands were still covered with snow, but that just made things all the more beautiful.

As I was headed westbound on the Toad River at only two hundred feet or so, I spotted a black spot on the snow in the middle of the channel. I knew instantly what it was, although I felt it was unusually early. I punched the intercom button. "Sharon, look at what's up ahead."

She put down our map and peered ahead, then shot me a dirty look. "Why didn't you let me bring my camera? I just knew this would happen."

"Because we're a hundred pounds over gross as it is with all our gas cans and stuff, and we just didn't have room."

She wasn't buying it, and to make matters worse she sensed that I was up to something. "So now what do you think you're doing?" she asked in a peeved voice.

"We'll stop and take a look at him, since I can't figure out why he's out so early."

I did a quick-stop, which is where you drop the collective control and stand a helicopter on its tail with the cyclic control and let the main rotor slow you down, and in the case of the Robinson R22 you're going from 90 knots to nothing in the matter of seconds. Once you've zeroed out, you shove the cyclic forward and level the ship, meanwhile lifting the collective to go into hover. It's quite a ride when you're going like a rocket and then suddenly stop...especially in front of a grizzly that's furious because somebody woke him up from his lunchtime nap. We had found a bear that had run down a moose on the river, fed on it, and was defending it with its spread-eagled body. Like Sharon said on the intercom, "He looks just like a big flying squirrel."

I still can't say whether a brown bear will *kung fu* with a helicopter, but I can tell you that a grizzly will certainly *charge* one. And it's a good thing you can fly backward in a flash, because otherwise this one would have smashed out the Plexiglas bubble to get at us. Holy crap did he get mad, and he must have definitely loved moose meat. He wouldn't back off no matter what I'd do and around and around we went until I decided to give up. Actually, it got pretty scary, and it's hard to believe how enraged a bear can become. ...*Which takes me back to the beginning of this book.*

I have always said Amie Huguenard's death shrieks in 2003 were the screams heard around the world. Her duplicitous boyfriend, Timothy Treadwell, was already pretty much eaten, since not much more than gnawed bones were found the day after he'd been attacked. Amie's awful fate was a forearm and a few bony fingers sticking out of some gooey debris as if she were beckoning someone, ala *Frankenstein* style, to unearth what little remained of her. Suddenly, the watering holes and greasy spoons all around Alaska were given a long winter's worth of, "Told you he'd get his ass eaten," to "Good enough for those two squirrel squeezers, since they weren't nothing but big phonies anyway. Nobody was poaching in Katmai, no matter what in hell the Hollywood crowd was saying."

I don't remember who first told me about Tim, but most likely it was someone at Katmailand, Inc., since it's the company that runs the restaurant, lodging, and transportation at Brooks Camp in the Katmai National Park and, thus, is integral to the daily operations of this wonderful place. Or it could have been Bill Sims, owner of the Newhalen Lodge near Lake Clark National Park, whom I've known a long time and would stop at my Lake Hood hangar and shoptalk about airplanes and sport fishing with me, since he sits right in the middle of the best of it. As I recall, he was one of the first people who helped Tim get started in Alaska, although I seriously doubt that he approved of his later antics such as kissing brown bears on the lips. Bill was once a hunting guide and would have known better than to establish, how should I say it, "intimate relationships" with them, since let's just say they tend to be rather fickle. In any case, Treadwell was a favorite topic around Anchorage and Kodiak for years and then doubly so when *People Magazine* published a stunning piece on him in 1994. All of a sudden, he was causing a great stir, upstaging all the known bear experts, and making them look like frightened schoolboys. This didn't set well with many Alaskans, as you can well imagine.

The mainstream media, the Internet, and about a million blogs are overloaded with stories about Treadwell and his unexpected accession into the bear world, with probably the most insightful articles being written by Craig Medred, the outdoor editor for the *Anchorage Daily News,* and a couple of writers of similar stripes. You can be sure of one thing, people will sit up and take notice when you start horsing around with half-ton bears and then end up as prime rib, red in the center, right along with a secondhand girlfriend. Tim came onto the scene something like a comet but left like a shooting star, and he won't be soon forgotten, or forgiven for that matter. Lots of folks still get worked up when you mention his name. The long and short of his thirteen or fourteen years of frolicking with brown bears, depending on when you think he actually got started at it, was a deadly charade of a California pothead who thought he was onto something big that would lead him to international fame and fortune. The problem you have, though, is not many used car salesmen ever get to be Rolls-Royce dealers, and that was Treadwell's problem. You only have to tell so many lies and pretty soon you lose most of your friends and make way too many enemies. As it turned out, his nonprofit organization, Grizzly People, was anything but, and nothing more than a slick hustle of various business bigwigs and Hollywood celebrities who had too much money and not enough brains to figure out what they were getting themselves into, with Patagonia, of all people, at the front of the line. I never cease to be amazed by the number of corporate bigwigs and movie stars who are smart enough to become multimillionaires but dumb enough to bet on born losers.

Tim more or less took possession, leastwise in his mind, of two of the best bear viewing spots in Alaska—Hallo Bay and Upper Kaflia Lake, both of which are along the Katmai Coast, and appointed himself high sheriff, chief bear expert, and resident photographer. Next, he took bear viewing to whole new levels by getting nose to nose with them and behaving a lot more like he was working with milk cows than man-eating predators that bite people's heads off when they get mad enough about something. The stage was set for a showdown at the O.K. Corral.

His sales pitch was that Katmai Park was rife with poachers who were determined to kill every last brown bear in Alaska, either to have them stuffed as trophies or sold for their gallbladders to those dirty rotten Asian aphrodisiac dealers. It was all complete nonsense. On the one hand, he was mooching big money from rich folks so he could safeguard a national treasure, yet on the other hand he was somehow convincing them that his pricy Alaskan expeditions were being copycatted by crooked poachers for next to nothing. "Yes sir, they sneak in, shoot the bears, then sneak right back out because there ain't nothing to it." For the life of me, I can't understand why someone didn't finally ask him, "Wait a minute, if it's costing you $50,000 a summer to protect the Katmai bears, how come it doesn't cost the poachers just as much to operate there? Something doesn't make sense here, since the damn bears can't be worth that much money."

If truth be told, the chances of poaching a brown bear in the Katmai Park aren't a lot better than knocking over Fort Knox. The minimum you would need is a $100,000 airplane, two guys, one of whom must be a good shot with a high-powered rifle that kicks so hard that it almost knocks your head off and the other a gorilla-like muscleman who can carry a hundred and fifty pound bear hide on his back two or three miles through an alder jungle where you can't see where you're going half the time. And this is all assuming you are a skilled bush pilot and were able to find a place to land and tie down your airplane where it would be safe for two or three days in the Katmai Coast's legendary windstorms. Also, since there's a veritable air force of government and privately-owned airplanes flying overhead every day, you must find a place where you won't be spotted as well, which isn't all that easy. Almost assuredly, someone will see you and call on their radio, "Roger, King Salmon Flight Service, we have a couple of guys over here that have a bear down and maybe you should give the Park Service a call. I'll give them a low pass and get the N-number on their airplane."

Increasing the chances that you will almost surely get caught, is it takes a few hours to the get the hide off a brown bear, since you must skin them every inch of the way. And lest you think all you have to do is squirrel yourself away in the bushes while you're doing your dirty work, try sliding a thousand pound animal across an uneven surface someday. It's impossible without having superhuman strength. Then to add to your various challenges, let's say you do, in fact, pull it off, so now what? Do you really think you can fool a taxidermist into believing you have a legal bear? All of them know a summer hide the instant they see one, and so they will turn you in to Fish and Game the first chance they get. Frankly, I believe bank robbery might be the better way to go, because at least you won't have to forfeit your airplane and pay a big fine besides, and I doubt the jail sentence would be any more severe either. Treadwell's stories about poaching were illusory at best.

No matter what he was told by the people who remained loyal to him, various park rangers, or the bear-viewing operators who often had confrontations with him on Kodiak Island, at Hallo Bay, or at Kaflia Lake he simply wouldn't stop pushing all the wrong buttons. He harassed different individuals, accused them of things they hadn't done, and, most of all, made a spectacle of himself by pretending he was some sort of Messiah who had the holy right to plunk himself down right in the middle of some of the most sensitive salmon streams in the world, which, of course, were crawling with brown bears ranging from sows with firstborns to behemoths that had been around for almost thirty years and were, let's say, usually cantankerous when it came to sharing their personal space with anything or anyone. No matter how many times he was told to stop his illegal activities, he would either laugh it off, lie about it, or cheat the moment no one was looking. What was so amazing, though, is he got away with it a lot longer than anyone could have guessed.

And here's where I can come in with some special insight, since at the time I was leasing and then selling my hangar to Katmailand, which was flying tourists back and forth on a daily basis between Anchorage and the Katmai Park under the exclusive agreement they hold with the federal government to operate the guest facilities at Brooks Camp. I'll never forget the day I was at my hangar doing the things that landlords ordinarily do and saw a pile of firewood stacked alongside my building. I'm a bit of a neat-freak and asked Katmailand's employees why on earth they were storing wood on my property, which I thought not only looked a little trashy but could be considered a fire hazard as well. "Oh, the Park Service won't let us cut any firewood and all the dead trees have to be left alone," they said, "so we have to fly wood in for our fireplaces." At the time, I knew about the monkeyshines Treadwell was pulling at Katmai, and yet here is a first class tourist operation that was central to the park's success and it couldn't whack up some firewood with a chainsaw when it needed some, which would undoubtedly be good for the surrounding forest and lessen the risk of someday having a fire right where no one wants one. It was okay with the National Park Service for Treadwell to be thumbing his nose at every rule in the book, but yet no one else dared chop up a dead tree for fear of prosecution. All I can say is I learned long ago if you don't want to deal with goofy people and their double standards don't do business with the U.S. government. Most of their policies will make you want to run from their offices, screaming and tearing off all your clothing because of how convoluted they can get.

On September 29, 2003, Treadwell and Amie Huguenard set up camp on Kaflia Lake for the last time. Both intended to stay a week and then head for Los Angeles once again with photography that could be used to fleece America over the looming extinction of the Alaskan brown bear. It was the same old rip-off that's been used countless times—first you invent a crisis, even though one doesn't exist, exaggerate the problem with people who don't know any better, then hit them up for money. "Please, please, help us save the bears before it's too late, because the poachers are killing them one after another." Unfortunately, things would turn out a lot differently this time, and I'm sadly reminded of an age-old adage—"Sometimes the hunter gets the bear, and sometimes the bear gets the hunter." Little did either know they would be dead in a couple of days, leaving Alaska, right along with the rest of the nation, inalterably changed for the rest of time. Two humans would be killed and eaten by an unknown number of bears, and then in turn two bears would be killed by humans, only to be eaten by other bears in a ghoulish twist of fate. Mother Nature never lets anything go to waste, especially in Alaska.

Tim couldn't have picked a worse place for their campsite, which was centered in a cobweb of bear trails leading to a salmon stream. But he had done that for a dozen years, despite being told innumerable times he was going to get himself into trouble. He hated guns, didn't use bear spray, and refused to take any sensible precautions with his life, let alone anyone else's. Brown bears were nothing more than big pussycats, he frequently said, and he'd never met one that he couldn't make back down. His showboating had always saved him before, so why should it fail him now? But that's precisely what happened.

I wouldn't mind it so much if it weren't for Amie. Tim got what he deserved—that doesn't mean I'm not sorry he's dead, but I suppose it's a lot like what my mother-in-law always says, "What're you gonna do?" The man wouldn't listen, and worse than that, he went through life believing he could cowboy his way through everything. His false bravado blew up in his face, and he begged for his life in such a way as to leave everything he'd said and done through the years in infamy. Frankly, begging Amie to save him with a frying pan is still too much for me to stomach. He had bragged he wasn't afraid of getting killed by a bear, but in the end that wasn't true at all. I learned long ago as a chief pilot and flight instructor it was always the hotdogs you had to watch out for, since they were forever flying off and killing themselves. It was the quiet ones you could depend on to bring themselves back in one piece.

I wrote early in this book that Amie didn't need to die at all, not if she'd known what to do in an emergency, and here's where Treadwell can be clearly blamed. It was one thing for him to be pulling all his shenanigans, since he was a big boy and knew the risks, but it was quite a different thing to get an innocent woman involved in his dangerous stunts. Selfish, stupid, and as irresponsible as you can get, that's exactly what it was. Why he didn't have a contingency plan to save her, or for that matter, the other women he'd taken to Hallo and Kaflia, I'll never know. His egomania and negligence are unforgivable.

First, almost no one else would have pitched camp where he did, but be that as it may, there was no excuse for him not having a backpacker's raft, an emergency locator transmitter, a flare gun, and a small bag of survival supplies ready for her instant use. In addition, he should have done a couple of dry runs with her so she understood what to do if he was ever taken down. "Amie, if I'm attacked, grab this stuff and get out into the lake. Don't try helping me, looking back, or running, just sneak away as quickly as possible. Turn on the emergency beacon and the Coast Guard in Kodiak will be over here with a helicopter in a flash regardless of the weather. You'll be safe and it will also give me my best chance for survival. Now let's practice what you must do." That's what a responsible person would have said and done, let alone a true outdoorsman, but sad to say Tim was neither. And so Amie had to die a thousand deaths, screaming her head off for Lord knows how long, but certainly long enough for her to have saved her own life instead.

 # NANOOK

MOST PEOPLE THINK ABOUT ALASKA when you mention polar bears, but the greatest number of them in North America are found along Hudson Bay, not far north of Minnesota. Churchill, Manitoba, which calls itself the Polar Bear Capital of the World, has now become famous for its tundra buggies that take tourists out along the Bay's coast to see them wandering around like cattle. Back in the 1970s, I used to see as many as sixty or seventy on a single flight when I'd fly from York Factory to Churchill, and I wouldn't have stood a chance if my engine had quit. Not because I couldn't have set my seaplane down safely, since there are lakes all over, but because there were so many bears it would have been like landing on an anthill. That was back in the days when Churchill's townspeople would literally go to war with them every summer, and it was every man for himself. They are ferocious predators that usually aren't one bit afraid of humans.

There's been this continuous debate as to which is the biggest bear, the polar or the brown, and then the added wrinkle of where the polar bear came from in the first place. Recordkeeping ostensibly has it that a brown on Kodiak Island once weighed in at 2,500 pounds and a 2,200-pound polar was shot in 1960 on Kotzebue Sound in Western Alaska, so let's just say that settles it. I have seen lots of both and there's no question in my mind the brown bear will usually run a little bigger than the polar, and well it should because of its better diet. You must remember that sometimes the brown has so much to eat it will only strip a spawning salmon for its brains and eggs and leave the rest to rot. Meanwhile, the polar has to bust its butt punching through snow and ice to catch one lousy seal in forty-below temperatures. Common sense will generally answer most scientific questions, although you wouldn't know it when you listen to how most of our bear experts come up with their answers.

It wasn't long ago that biologists were sure the polar was a separate species of bear from the brown and they couldn't, among other things, interbreed in the wild. *Wrong!* In May of 2006, an Idaho hunter named Jim Martel shot a grizzly-polar hybrid on Banks Island in the Northwest Territories, which after a lot of hand wringing and disbelief by various wannabe bear authorities, proved by DNA to be a true crossbreed between a grizzly father and polar mother. Interestingly, the Inuit of Sachs Harbour, who had guided Martel on the perfectly legal hunt, had thought all along it was a hybrid bear. But what the hell do they know, since they have only lived up there several thousand years and told traditional stories about this phenomenon since day one? I never cease to be amazed by the experts who instantly dismiss what indigenous people have to say about wildlife they've lived with since the beginning of time.

How the polar evolved is a good question. Scientists say that genetics prove that browns and polars are closely related, yet they argue the polar is a separate species that somehow was once a brown that turned white because it was long ago blocked off by big glaciers and then adapted to living on the Arctic Ocean. Just how these glaciers barricaded the top of the world and kept the polars in and the browns out somehow escapes my brain's ability to wrap around what they are talking about, particularly when in the next breath they pontificate about the Bering land bridge and humans populating Alaska at the same time (10,000 to 20,000 years ago), when it has also been proved by fossil records the polar's teeth morphed into something different than what's found in a brown's mouth. If I haven't lost you with all this, everybody may very well be better off listening to the legends the Inuit elders tell about the evolution of the polar bear, since those stories are no more farfetched than what our scientists are telling us. In my simpleminded view, you should think comets, solar flares, and supervolcanoes when you talk about species changes and let it go at that.

My first polar bear was one that I never saw, but it still got me cussed out by the guy everyone in Churchill called the Shell man. I had flown there from Gods Lake, which is an aptly named fishing hotspot in Northern Manitoba, and landed on a small lake not far from an old World War II airport, which was mostly abandoned at the time. It was the last place where you could buy any fuel for a long way around and was about as good as it got when it came to bush flying in Northern Canada. You radioed the flight service station, gave them your estimated time of arrival, and asked that fuel be brought down to you. "Roger, nine-six-Bravo, and would you like one barrel or two?" they'd ask. You made your choice, landed, and then waited at the end of a dirt road for the Shell dealer to show up in his pickup with a barrel or so of avgas, a hand pump, and a funnel. Up on the wing you would go, he'd pump and you'd fill your tanks, then off you would go again. The problem was that it usually took an hour or so for him to get there, and so you would wander around killing time while waiting. On my first flight into Churchill, it hadn't occurred to me the seaplane base was crawling with polars that were killing time as well.

I wandered up the dusty road and was surprised by the dwarf spruce and tundra bushes that covered the area, since it hadn't looked quite so thick from above. It was a perfect summer day but I'd forgotten my bug dope, so I was flapping my arms like a drunken goose by the time I got a few hundred feet away from my airplane. Finally, I ran into a couple of boarded-up shacks right beside the road, but, strangely, both looked like porcupines with bad haircuts because there were so many long nails sticking out of their doors and window shutters. I started putting two and two together and headed back to the lake as fast as I could go. I'd left my bear gun behind and suddenly knew that had been a big mistake.

I stopped the moment I reached my airplane and stared at its cowling and fuselage. *Who in hell has been throwing mud at my one-eighty?* I wondered. I was pissed but then took a second look. Paw marks. There were muddy bear tracks all over my floats, paw prints on top of the engine cowling and along the sides of the fuselage, including the windows, and they were all still sopping wet. Godalmighty, I almost jumped out of my skin, and it didn't take me but a few seconds to open the pilot's door and pull out my gun. I was scared because the bear couldn't be far away, but it still hadn't dawned on me what had *really* happened. I was idiotically wondering what a black bear was doing so far north. Like Bugs Bunny says, "What a maroon!"

A few minutes later, I heard something coming and then watched as the Shell man wheeled around and backed up to my plane with his pickup. He jumped out and eyeballed my rifle and me. "What'd you do, have to chase one of them bastards out of here?" he asked. I explained what had happened, then watched as he peered at the muddy footprints on my airplane. "You're goddamn lucky you didn't get yourself killed or your airplane torn apart, aye. You don't go walking around here unless you're crazy, because you're going to get yourself ate. Bloody Christ, there's a dozen of them at the dump everyday, and it ain't even safe to walk around town." That's how I first learned about the polar bears of Churchill, along with the fascinating history of Hudson Bay.

At the same time the first English settlement, Jamestown, Virginia, was being colonized; Henry Hudson started searching for the Northwest Passage, which had been England's pigheaded figment of imagination since the discovery of America. He first explored the Hudson River, sailing as far as Albany, and then on his last voyage in 1610 found his way into Hudson Bay after surviving the Titanic-sized icebergs and the sixty-foot tides of the ocean straits lying below Greenland. Sailing on, he followed the east coast of the bay and discovered several islands during his passage into James Bay, where he got himself icebound on its southern shore until June of the following year. When the icepack finally thawed, he wanted to continue westward, undoubtedly convinced because of his navigational use of the astrolabe, the compass, and the crude maps of the time that he was well on his way to the Pacific Ocean. His crew was starving and dying of scurvy, wanted no part of it, and mutinied against him, taking over his ship, the *Discovery*, and setting his son, John, seven loyal sailors, and him adrift in a little boat in the middle of nowhere, never to be seen or heard from again. All poor Henry got for his troubles was his name plastered forevermore on the world's maps, which was pretty scant payment for being sentenced to death by men who had pledged their allegiance to him.

A few surviving crewmen and the *Discovery* finally sailed back to England, where they were to be hanged for mutiny, but the British Crown and its Admiralty, ever on the search for the least clue to the fabled Northwest Passage, never quite got around to it and eventually some of the very same crewmen sailed for the Arctic once again. It has long been speculated that Henry Hudson had really been on a top-secret mission and England never wanted to risk that anything would ever be revealed to France and Spain, who were its bitter enemies. Yes, there were even spies back then who would sneak into court and listen to what was being said.

The mutineers had returned with stories of bloodthirsty Indians and Eskimos, hungry polar bears, but the finest beaver pelts in the world as well. Sixty years later, the British Crown granted the newly incorporated Hudson's Bay Company a complete monopoly on all the fur trade in Rupert's Land, which represented over one-third of Canada and a little of the United States, or in other words, all of the North American lands where the rivers flowed north. That included the Red River in Minnesota, for example, so the Hudson's Bay Company actually controlled over 1.5 million square miles, making it the largest landowner on earth. In 1682 it built a fort and trading post named Fort Nelson on the southwestern corner of the bay as its headquarters and started making money hand over fist, which upset the hell out of the French because they felt Rupert's Land belonged to them.

In 1684, a French naval force attacked and destroyed Fort Nelson, which forced the English to move a little south, construct a new fort named York Factory on the Hayes River, and get back into business. France attacked again in 1697 and defeated them in the largest naval battle ever fought in the Arctic and renamed the place Fort Bourbon. Finally in 1713, the Treaty of Utrecht chopped up North America between the British, the French, and the Spanish and the Hudson's Bay Company was able to carry on with their fur trading until it abandoned York Factory in 1957. It still has department stores throughout Canada and is the oldest corporate business in North America, as well as one of the oldest in the world.

The Hudson's Bay Company built a second fort and trading post at the present site of Churchill in 1717, which was later replaced by stone fortifications in 1731, although it took forty additional years to reach completion. The French weren't quite finished with the British yet, and so in 1782 they attacked Churchill as a diversionary tactic to keep the Royal Navy spread thin and assure its defeat around the world. England had just lost the Revolutionary War, which later had turned into a world war with France and Spain siding with us, and since the French weren't beyond kicking a guy when he was down, what better way than razing a perfectly good fort and ruining the Brit's fur trade? Eventually, the fort was given back, restored, and still stands today. Click a Web search engine for *Fort Prince of Wales* if you want to see an aerial view of it, and the last I knew if you dug under some of its ramparts you could still find old cannon balls.

Hudson Bay's history interested me so much that I eventually read a narrative of an 1819 expedition led by a Royal Navy officer named John Franklin in search of the Northwest Passage. The British Admiralty ordered him to explore the Canadian Arctic from York Factory to Great Slave Lake with longboats, float down the Coppermine River, and then sail east along the coast of the "Polar Sea," as it was called back then. The idea was to map everything on the way back to Hudson Bay, however harebrained that scheme might seem to us nowadays. As it worked out, he had lost eleven of his twenty men by the time he made it back to England in 1822. Starvation, scurvy, cannibalism, freezing to death, murder, he'd seen it all by the time he got back home.

He wrote a bestseller about his adventures and became known as "the man who ate his boots," but, sadly, the bitter lessons he'd learned didn't set in very well. In 1845, he left with three Royal Navy ships for one last shot at the Northwest Passage, but he and his 128 men disappeared forever. It has been long believed the expedition was frozen in somewhere near King William Island up above the middle of Canada and never got free of the sea ice again. *Where's a little global warming when you need it?* In any case it's thought that everyone died from scurvy, lead poisoning from poor quality tin cans, murder, cannibalism, and whatever else that takes place when humans are lost, hypothermic, and starving to death. The English could never get it in their heads that to survive in the Arctic, you must live and dress like the Inuit. They always thought that was beneath their dignity.

Franklin's detailed account of York Factory stuck in my mind for some reason, in particular his description of a small chapel where he was asked to give a religious sermon following his arrival. The English were very devout back then, and it was customary for the locals to ask a visitor as important as a naval officer to preach to them. He was somewhat annoyed when he saw the podium that he was to use, as it was painted red, yellow, and green, which was sacrilegious as far as he was concerned. Nevertheless, he did what they asked and came away happy with the rapt attention that was paid him by the Whites and Swampy Cree who had attended his service, and then wrote nice things about the factor who ran the place (HBC trading posts were always managed by men who were called factors). Shortly thereafter, he and his men happily set off up the Hayes River for Great Slave Lake, but his joy didn't last long. The Hayes is big, fast, and wide, and they were soon forced to unload everything they could do without. One such item was a small brass cannon, which leads me to the story of the first polar bear I certainly *did* see, and much closer than I wanted.

In the 1960s, I was flying out of St. Cloud, Minnesota, for a boss who had a Beechcraft Model 18 with a Conrad Conversion, which was a World-War-II-era airplane with two Pratt & Whitney radial engines and modifications that gave you the gross weight of 10,200 pounds and more speed than the ordinary model. It was a big, low-wing, taildragger that could carry eight people, plus crew, and was the Lear Jet of its time, but, oh, was it tough to fly. Taildraggers are always troublemakers on takeoffs and landings, but when they have two engines, they are twice as bad. It's funny I didn't crash and burn, but that's another story for a different time. At any rate, my boss had me flying fishermen into Northern Canada where I became friends with the Swampy Cree who were working as fishing guides at a couple of fly-in lodges. Their stories of York Factory fascinated me.

Since the Swampy Cree had done business there for almost 300 years and it had been only closed ten, my brand-new friends knew the place well. They told me wonderful stories about how they had shot the foaming rapids of the tributary rivers running into the Hayes and then their long runs down into Hudson Bay. They told me about the skies turning black with migrating geese and the tidewater creeks turning orange with sea-run brook trout. They told me about the polar bears and the seals living on the flat shorelines. Best of all, they told me where I could land with a seaplane beside some hunting shacks and how to find the guides to take me out. I desperately wanted to see the place.

Finally, I flew there with a friend in a borrowed Cessna floatplane, and we weren't disappointed in what we found, although I almost wrecked the airplane. My new friends had forgotten to tell me that Hudson and James Bays make up the largest inland sea in the world and its ten-foot tides tear at York Factory day and night. Holy crap, did I ever come close to busting the wings off a perfectly good airplane, and everything would have been lost but for a roar much like a freight train.

It was late afternoon when I circled the shacks I'd been told about and saw some boats and motors tied to the shoreline a little way upriver from York Factory itself. The Swampy Cree from Shamattawa had come down Gods River to hunt and would take my friend and me out for as long as we wanted. I landed in a side channel of the Hayes that looked deep enough and taxied to the riverbank beside the boats. Several men met us and helped tie the Cessna onto pilings that had been pounded into the shallower water. Hudson Bay is infamous for its nasty weather and I wanted the plane protected from any windstorms. We carried our gear to one of the shacks, rolled out our sleeping bags, and got ready for supper. Autumn reds and yellows had highlighted the willows along the river, and the air was filled with fall fragrances and the calls of white geese.

We ate and then sat around an open campfire and got to know each other. One of the Shamattawas was a young chief whose high brown cheekbones, raven hair, and dark gleaming eyes gave him a classic, sovereign face, and we hit it off because he trapped in the wintertime and I understood the hardships he faced. We shared stories about the work it took to catch beaver under the ice and how to make snow sets for fox and mink. He told me about having wolf packs trailing him as he snowshoed along his trapline and how his grandfathers had told him they were man-killers before his ancestors got guns. He was someone who was still living off the land, and so he thought of himself as an essential part of the Earth Mother.

Later, since we were so tired from flying all day, my friend and I crawled into our bunks and quickly fell asleep. I remember hearing the distant whispers of the river...but it seemed like part of an odd dream. *Then I woke up!* The whispers had become a waterfall, and the roar was as deafening as a train.

"Hey, wake up. What in hell is that?" I shouted across the room.

There were the sounds of someone waking from a deep sleep in the middle of the night. "Christ, I don't know...what's wrong?" my friend answered in a froglike voice.

I found my flashlight and turned it on, then started pulling on my clothes like a madman. "Come on, hurry up—we gotta check the airplane. There must be some kind of weather moving in."

I dove out of the door almost on a dead run with my friend right behind me, but the first thing that struck me was the weather seemed just fine. There wasn't a breath of wind, only some frost on the weeds and leaves in my beaming flashlight. Other than that it was moonless, you could see a million miles. Suddenly, I realized it had to be the Hayes River, but what in hell was it, Noah's flood? Little did I know how close to the truth I had come.

We ran down the footpath that led to the river and couldn't believe our eyes. The Hayes was running backward and rising by the minute, and I had never seen so much floodwater. It was my first time around an ocean tide, and you had better leave lots of slack in the tiedown ropes you use or it's bye-bye airplane. The wings of the Cessna I had borrowed looked as if both were on the nocks of a big bowstring, and I had only seconds to do something.

If there's one thing you learn about flying in the Alaskan and Canadian bush it's that you don't even walk down the street without carrying a pocketknife and waterproof matches. What you have on you are the only things that you will have left if you sink your seaplane, so it better be in your pant's pockets if you're ever lucky enough to make it ashore. Forget about your survival kit, because you won't have time to find it. Going tits up in a floatplane gives you little more than the chance to prove how long you can hold your breath and how far you can swim.

I had a buck knife and went after the right-hand tiedown rope like Jack the Ripper, knowing full well I'd be flipped into the air. Both floats were almost submerged, so the instant the rope let loose the airplane would jerk sideways. I was going for the ride of my life whether I liked it or not, and then afterward I'd have to decide how to get over to the opposite side to save myself, right along with the airplane. One mistake and I'd join Franklin in his underwater grave.

I looped my left arm around the top half of the wing strut, held on for dear life, and cut the rope. *Bang!* The top half of the tiedown rope snapped against the bottom of the wing and I instantly got flipped off my feet and dangled in the air as if I were a body bag. Next, I fell down the wing strut, slammed into the fuselage, and flopped against the front float struts running up to the engine firewall.

Suddenly there was so much light!

But I didn't have time to figure out why because I had to get over to the other side as fast as possible. The left wingtip was dipping into the water and there was no time to spare. I wrapped my arms and legs around the front spreader bar running between both floats and took another circus ride, except I slid crosswise underneath the airplane this time. *Splash!* Now I slammed against the far float, which was almost sunken. I spit out a mouthful of icy water, pulled myself up by grabbing the left wing strut, and went after the opposite tiedown rope as if Jack had been a onetime killer. I had a minute, maybe two.

Wham! The second rope split in two and the airplane nearly threw me off again, but then it splashed level with the river where it belonged. After that, I felt it being pulled backward with its rudder and elevators sticking into the riverbank's brush. I had given my friend my flashlight and told him to hang onto the tail rope when I'd started cutting the main tiedowns, but now as I looked backward I saw the chief had come to help with what looked like his whole tribe. There were flashlights everywhere, which explained why I'd suddenly had so much light. I stood there a moment and didn't know what to say, and then started shivering because I'd gotten so cold and soaking wet, or maybe because I knew how close I'd come. Finally, I walked off the float I was standing on and helped retie everything to trees above the high-tide mark. Everyone was looking sideways at me as if I were some kind of god...or a complete idiot, but I didn't know which. Then I noticed the chief and a couple of his men were carrying guns. He walked up to me when we were done with the airplane.

"Okay, I talk to men that here when you fly in. They make bad mistake not tell you about tide."

"Listen, it's my fault and I should have known better. It's not like I couldn't have seen what would happen if I'd only looked around."

"No, you guest here, so we sorry."

By the look on his face, even in the fitful shadows of so many flashlights, I knew there was no sense in arguing. He was someone who regularly made decisions, and this was a matter of pride on his part. The Swampy Cree depended on bush pilots for their medical emergencies and tribal business with the Canadian government, so they looked at them as unique individuals. Airplanes had fascinated them from the very beginning, and the men and women who flew them were special in their eyes. His men had let him down.

We started back to the shacks and I wanted to change the subject. "How come you're carrying a gun?" I asked.

The chief never so much as broke his stride. "Polar bear smell us and not safe here. They hunt seal all time on river."

I realized I had made another big mistake, since the trees and brush along the Hayes were thick enough to hide a bear whether it was white or not. You wouldn't know you were in any danger until it was too late, especially at night, and if the Shamattawas were scared, that was good enough for me. I started shining my flashlight left and right, helping the chief light up our surroundings.

The next morning, I couldn't believe my eyes when we walked back to where the airplane was parked. I could now walk under the bottoms of the floats because both were beached so high on the riverbank. As a flatland pilot, I had learned an important lesson when it came to flying around ocean water, and I realized that I wouldn't be leaving whenever I wanted. I would have to wait until the tide came back in, at least to the extent of being able to power back down into the water and having it deep enough to taxi around safely. There were rocks and snags everywhere.

The chief took my friend and me downriver to hunt geese, and as we passed York Factory I saw that it looked just like John Franklin had described it when he'd first seen it. To me, it was like traveling back in time, and I was really looking forward to stopping when we came back upriver. The chief said an old man was staying there who would show us around.

We motored nearly into Hudson Bay itself, then turned into a cutbank the tides had washed out and tied our boat to some bushes. I couldn't believe my eyes and ears. There were snow and blue geese everywhere, and they were making so much noise you couldn't hear yourself think. Snowstorms of them were wheeling over our heads and landing on the open stretches to feed on the grasses that grew there. This was their stopover point where they were resting and feeding for their long flights south as they had done since antediluvian times, and the Swampy Cree had hunted them for almost as long. The coming winter had chased them off the barren lands hundreds of miles north and they were tired and hungry. The chief laughed at my friend's and my open-mouthed amazement.

Hunting them was no more than a matter of sneaking through the scattered brush and waiting until a flock almost landed on your head, or if you were a meat hunter for the very reason the Shamattawas were there, you simply killed two or three on the ground with a single shot, at least if you could get everything lined up right. There was nothing sporting about it, other than if you wanted to flare them off and shoot them on the wing. I started feeling guilty, since it wasn't even fair, but then the chief reminded me that his village needed all the geese we could shoot. He and his men had come a long way downriver and faced another dangerous trip back, and they wanted to return home with all the geese they could carry. His men were back at the shacks saving the feathers, salting, smoking, and preserving the meat however they could, and he was perfectly happy with two white men using up their shotgun shells rather than his. The opportunity for the Shamattawas to earn money to buy anything, let alone shells, was very limited at the time, and I've learned their prospects haven't changed much since. There are currently about 1,100 people in Shamattawa, Manitoba, and the average of one in four has tried committing suicide. The modern world has no idea of the crushing isolation and poverty of a subsistence lifestyle in the middle of nowhere in this day and age, especially when the Swampy Cree are even condemned now for earning a little money by fur trapping.

After a few hours, we picked up all our geese and ran back upriver to York Factory and beached our boat. It was a slog to climb the steep muddy riverbank to the flat stretch that led to the old trading post, but afterward the ground was high and dry. There were numerous outbuildings and it was more of a fort back in the days of Franklin, but now I saw all that remained was the great warehouse square where most of the money-making activity had taken place in the past. Regardless, it was like stepping into the past.

The building faced the river with a middle edifice almost three-stories high, then there were long structures of equal dimensions on each side of the center section. Each of these wings had four large windows on the bottom and the same on top, while the middle looked more like a courthouse with its churchlike main entrance, slanted roof, and bell tower. It was clad in weathered, white siding and its different roofs were covered with lead sheets the same as modern shingles. Everything looked rundown as one would expect, yet you couldn't help but feel impressed by its towering presence. An elderly man stepped out to greet us and introduced himself as the caretaker the Canadian government had sent there to protect the many artifacts that had been left behind by the Hudson's Bay Company. Needless to say, he was glad to see us, since he'd hardly seen a human face all summer.

We walked in and the first thing I saw was the old fur press that had been used to flatten beaver pelts into bales suitable for storing one on top of another in ships' cargo holds. It struck me as looking a lot like an oversized Ben Franklin printing press with its wonderful old wood and rusty fittings. Next, I looked at how the building had been cleverly constructed of hewn timbers that flexed on the heaving permafrost of the different seasons, which is what had destroyed the brick and stone work of the earlier construction. Ship builders had been employed to construct the place and their craftsmanship was clearly evident, particularly on the horizontal and vertical beams that held everything together. Tree trunks and their roots had been dug out and then hewn into ninety-degree angles to fasten everything together in such a way as to withstand the freezing-and-thawing soil. The technology was the same as that used in wooden sailing ships to survive the pounding of heavy seas.

Then we were shown the brass cannon that had just been found along the Hayes River and returned to York Factory to add to its relics. It was fireplug-sized and I was stunned at its beauty. It was just as John Franklin had described it as he'd told his men to remove it from his longboat and cache it ashore in 1819, along with the rest of what his expedition couldn't carry up the Hayes, let alone all the way to Great Slave Lake. Once again, the British could never get used to the long distances, the white-water rivers, and the backbreaking portages of the Canadian Arctic, let alone its sub-zero temperatures, which ultimately cost them countless lives.

We wandered through the whole facility, which was actually a large, H-shaped warehouse as much as anything. It was easy to imagine the Swampy Cree coming in with their furs and trading for the Hudson's Bay point blankets (colorful wool blankets), knives, axes, and what were usually called Northwest guns, all the things essential for carrying on with their hunting-and-gathering lifestyles in Northern Canada. York Factory alone accounted for 20,000 trade muskets in its early history, with the standard exchange of twenty beaver pelts each. One could almost hear the factor shouting at his men as they carried merchandise back and forth in the building, baled beaver pelts, cut firewood to keep the place warm, and rowed their lighters out into the bay to the sailing ships waiting at anchor, since they could only come so close because of the dangerous tidewaters off the mouth of the Hayes River. York Factory was more or less the administrative headquarters for the Hudson's Bay Company for 273 years, and its considerable size reflected its importance to England and its economy.

There were cannon balls, stained glass windows, blacksmith tools, stoves, kettles, dishes, and valuable antiques of every kind scattered around, since Parks Canada had just started preserving the place as a heritage site. We took our time and looked at everything, and then I got the surprise of my life as I walked into the building's little chapel. There it was in all its living glory—the colorful podium Franklin had given his sermon from, and it was as if I could hear his ghost speaking. Of all the floatplane trips I'd taken in my life, this one would be the most unforgettable...for more reasons than one.

We walked outside and examined the outside of the building, and I was in for another surprise. Outlined on the walls were the silhouettes of polar bear hides that clearly had been nailed there for generations, leaving their giant flying-squirrel shapes forever etched on the weathered siding. I knew polars were big, but not that big, and although there was little doubt in my mind these had been put up there because of their exceptional size, it was still a real eye opener to see the enormous dimensions of their bodies. I was familiar with black bears, of course, having lived around them for a long time at that point, but it would have taken three or four blacks to make up just one of the bears on the wall. I began to realize why the chief and his men had been so jumpy when I'd ran off to save the Cessna. Running into one of these along the river at night would pose some real problems, regardless of the weapon you were carrying.

Our day ended with our return to the boat landing where our airplane was parked and hauling the geese we'd shot to the hunting shacks. The chief's men set about cleaning them and making an evening meal for us, since we'd had nothing but pilot bread, cold meat, and candy bars all day. After everyone had eaten, we sat around an outdoor fire again and talked about the exciting things we'd seen, especially at York Factory. I enjoyed telling the Shamattawas about Franklin's disastrous 1819 expedition and the loss of over half of his men in his attempt to find the Northwest Passage. The chief translated my stories to his men who couldn't understand English, and I saw them trading glances and nodding their heads upon learning how foolish the British had been in challenging the Arctic with the kinds of clothing, equipment, and boats they had used, topped off by their abysmal hunting and fishing skills.

Finally, I turned to the chief and said, "This is one of the most interesting places in the world and without a doubt has the best goose hunting anywhere. You have a real gold mine here, and I could help you build some better places for people to stay. We could advertise in the Chicago and Minneapolis newspapers and in a few years you'd make so much money you wouldn't have to do anything."

Undoubtedly, the chief had a better grasp than me on what was important in life, or at least in *his* life. "Me do nothing now," he answered with a clever smile.

It took me a moment to understand that it made little sense to go through all the hassle when he already had the peace and tranquility I was talking about, and my philosophy on life was rather flawed. Everyone had a good laugh at my expense.

The next morning we went hunting again, and it was even better than the day before, since I could tell the weather was changing for the worse, which the geese knew as well. We shot ourselves silly and then slowed down simply to watch the whirlwinds of geese spiraling down over our heads. It was hard to imagine there were places left in North American where wildlife was so abundant you simply couldn't count their numbers. My friend and I took our time, picked our wing shots, and enjoyed our moment in a very special place where we were also helping men we'd come to admire for the work they were putting in for their village.

Suddenly, the chief, who didn't have a gun, broke out in his native language. I don't understand Cree but immediately looked to my right, following his gaze. I had never seen anything like it. There was a polar bear galloping right toward us, and we'd missed seeing it coming up the shoreline. I didn't like how close it had gotten to us, and we had no time to do anything but run for our boat. And here I'd thought hunting geese at York Factory was duck-soup simple.

Unquestionably, the bear had smelled our geese and us and was homing in on the smell of food, which is the exact reason why so many polars gather at York Factory every summer. They often feed on ducks, geese, and their eggs, and Hudson Bay is one of best habitats in the world for waterfowl, let alone bears. The chance to save ourselves was to leave our dead geese behind and let the polar have them, since it would almost certainly stop, start feeding, and give us time to get away. It only required a single glance between the three of us before we started running. Twelve-gauge shotguns loaded with birdshot aren't good bear guns under any circumstance, leastways not unless you let them get within a few feet, which isn't smart with horse-sized bears.

We pushed into the Hayes River and then motored back and forth looking at the bear, since neither my friend or I had ever seen one close up. I grew up on a small farm with bad-tempered bulls and boar pigs, so I had learned at a young age to judge animals by their size and temperament, because one mistake meant your life, or at least a life-threatening injury. This animal was at least eight-hundred pounds, but what surprised me was its lack of fear. It could have cared less that we were there, and it started eating our geese one after another. Its focused aggression, slinky look, and fearlessness left an impression I've never forgotten.

I flew away the following day with a wilderness experience almost no one else ever gets, and the much the better for it. Polar bears take no prisoners.

THE HIGH ARCTIC

THE LAST PERSON KILLED BY A POLAR BEAR in Churchill, Manitoba, was in 1983, one year after its residents had built their "jail" for the annoying "shoplifters" that were often found walking into all the wrong places, the Royal Canadian Legion Club for example. Rumor has it a bartender shouted, "Get out of here, you're not a member," and the bear left.

A Native-Canadian decided the freezer of the Churchill Hotel, which had just burned to the ground, must still have lots of goodies inside. He was right and loaded up with the beefsteaks he'd found, only to run into a much bigger thief. Short of smearing yourself with bacon grease, I can't think of anything worse than walking around Hudson Bay with raw meat stuffed into your pockets. Sadly, the man was savagely killed, which resulted in the polar bear being tracked down and killed as well, which has happened all too often since Churchill was first settled so long ago. It's only been in recent times the townspeople have formed a posse that uses tranquilizer darts on nuisance bears, locks them in cages, and holds them hostage until the pack ice is such that they can be set free. In addition, under situations like a sow with cubs, some are sling-loaded away with helicopters and released where they can't return, leastwise not for a season. Interestingly, the bears were fed in their cages at first, but the following year they tried breaking *into* jail, so that ended that nonsense. Now they aren't even given bread and water...well, water is okay, but nothing else.

Polars have this quizzical, laid-back look on their faces that fools everyone into believing they're just big cuddly teddy bears that present little danger to human beings. They snoop around at a measured pace, seldom run at high speeds, and then only for short distances, and exhibit a curiosity in things that seems strangely precautious for supposedly being so ferocious. They are famous for walking up to a Churchill tundra buggy, standing with their front paws against its flat sides, and staring up at the passengers with innocent gazes. Don't let them fool you, since they are the world's most cunning predators, and there's no other species that can survive on the frozen Arctic Ocean all on its own.

People can't begin to understand the polar bear until they know what the Arctic Ocean is all about, which is actually a gigantic mishmash of the Barents Sea, the Beaufort Sea, the Chukchi Sea, the Greenland Sea, Hudson Bay, the Kara Sea, the Laptev Sea, the Siberian Sea, and the White Sea, along with a host of other bays and straits that are too numerous to mention. Collectively, everything totals something the size of Russia, except its dimensions are even larger and much more complex because there are so many Hawaiian-sized islands like those above Canada's mainland that cover the top of the world as well. Even today, despite our satellites and everything else, the Arctic Ocean remains the greatest mystery on earth. For example, if you simultaneously weigh yourself at home and on Hudson Bay, you weigh less up north. Our best scientists can't explain why Hudson Bay has less gravity than the rest of the world, yet they are sure the North Pole is melting. Maybe they're right, but I urge you to be suspicious, since how come they can figure out one thing and not the other?

I've flown over the pack ice on a few occasions, but I had the good fortune of having a friend who was the first man to land a wheeled airplane at the North Pole, a feat that won him international fame and a huge memorial that stands today at Yellowknife, Northwest Territories. Don Braun, without question, was the greatest bush pilot who ever lived. And what's so amazing is he died of old age in St. Cloud, Minnesota, my hometown for twenty years, rather than having crashed and burned like so many of his contemporaries, never to be seen again. I got to know him well and listened to his stories for innumerable hours. No one knew more about the Arctic than him, and why not, since he was the one who was flying all the scientists around when they first began their experiments at the North Pole back in the late 1960s. Without him, they couldn't have gotten there in the first place.

The Arctic Ocean stays largely frozen year round with an icepack averaging ten feet thick, but it might be two-feet thick in one place and sixty-feet thick in another. Its water is less saline than the world's other oceans because of the inflow from countless freshwater rivers and streams and the lack of evaporation because of the extreme cold. Overall, it's a relatively shallow ocean, running roughly 3,500 feet deep, but what's *not* well understood is its perpetual motion, the ubiquitous shifting that rotates the icepack counterclockwise around the top of the world. The location of the North Pole never changes, but the ice covering it always does, or in much simpler terms, if you land at the pole one day you won't be there the next. The icepack will have carried you some distance away. Humans have had a hard time grasping this phenomenon, but the polar bears love it. No matter what time of year, the Arctic Ocean is a colossal icemaker (it even sounds like one), splitting into open water in some places, which are called leads, and piling up into long pressure ridges in others, which afterward migrate and break into icebergs where the seawater becomes comparatively ice free in such places as the North Atlantic. The process never stops, and never will.

This sets up the all-important relationship between the polar bear and its food source. The constant shifting, splitting, crashing, grinding, and piling up of the sea ice let bearded and ringed seals thrive under the ice, regardless of the time of year. There are always places for them to surface and breath, even though the pack ice appears to be nothing but one big parking lot. There's just one problem...the polar bear can smell their secret blowholes from miles away and knows just how to sneak up, pounce through the snow and ice, and kill them. It's how they make their living, and they're very good at it.

It took almost until the twentieth century before many of the world's most celebrated experts stopped believing in the "Open Polar Sea," which, of course, is the reason Sir John Franklin and his men were lost as I mentioned in the preceding chapter. From the time of Henry Hudson's exploration of Hudson Bay in 1610 until 1895 when a couple of Norwegian explorers had been icebound for two years in their ship, *Fram*, did the baloney of an ice-free North Pole leave the mindset of so many eminent scientists. Finally, it started dawning on everyone the Arctic Ocean is always frozen, its pack ice floats on powerful ocean currents, and it often breaks into open leads that get slammed shut by windstorms before you can sail through them. It's the world's most unforgiving and dangerous place, which was what Don Braun was facing when he was asked to fly there.

In the late 1960s, a Canadian-led team of scientists wanted to know more about the North Pole, but there was just one small problem, how in hell to get there. Early twentieth-century explorers, Frederick Cook and Robert Peary, had each said he'd made it to the pole with the help of Eskimos and dogs, but it was quickly discovered that Cook was an unrepentant fraud and couldn't have gotten there like he'd said and Peary had mysteriously sprouted wings somewhere around 150 miles south of the pole where he could seldom dogsled a dozen miles a day to suddenly zipping along as if he were the Looney Tunes road runner, despite all the leads and pressure ridges that stood in his way. I'll paraphrase something Don Braun told me about their claims of conquering the North Pole, "Gall darn it, those two would've had to mush about a million miles to get around the open leads and ice ridges that circle the pole. It ain't possible they made it, and I had a hard enough time getting there and back with an airplane."

The dangers Don faced when he was asked to land at the pole were almost incomprehensible. Fortunately, he'd been flying the High Arctic, including landing on its desolate islands and vast icepack since the 1950s, but that had been with modern, ski-equipped airplanes. Suddenly, he was asked to fly a research team with all of its gear to the North Pole in a 44,000-pound twin-engine airplane called the Bristol Freighter, an ugly duckling if there ever was one, or maybe better described as 50,000 rivets flying in close formation. Its good points were it was a frisky British short-field airplane that had a clamshell nose that opened so you could haul things as big as bulldozers. Its bad points were it was a World War II taildragger with tricky engines and couldn't be put on skis. Don had a hell of a decision to make, and one with a dozen or so lives at stake.

Don had long believed an airstrip could be found at the North Pole where the Bristol Freighter could safely land, but only after a smaller, single-engine airplane on skis had been used to hopscotch north so he would have time to find a long stretch of smooth ice thick enough to support twenty-two tons. The plan had always been to use the military airbase at Alert, which is on the tip of Ellesmere Island 520 miles from the pole, and work north from there setting up fuel caches and navigation transmitters so he could safely work his way along in his quest for the Holy Grail. But time and work had always gotten in the way, at least until May of 1967.

He landed at Alert to pick up a load of helicopter fuel destined for Greenland, but got the biggest surprise of his life. A seven-man team of scientists were waiting for him to fly them to the North Pole. They said two ski-planes would be along shortly to assist them and everything had been pre-approved by Don's employer. ...Well, leastways there's one good thing about this, he told himself, I don't have to worry about finding any maps because there's ain't any, right along with a magnetic compass.

It's impossible to map the frozen Arctic Ocean because it changes every day. Winter and summer, the icepack breaks into open leads and piles into pressure ridges, which then freeze into new ice that is forever on the move in one direction or the other, but generally in a cyclonic twist around the top of the earth. There's nothing to map but an undulating, snowy bleakness broken by black leads that may or may not be solid ice. One never knows until you try walking on them.

The second nightmare a pilot faces when he or she flies in the Arctic is the North Pole and the North Magnetic Pole are in two different locations. Translated, this means if you leave Ellesmere Island and head to where the earth spins on its axis you must fly north, but if you wish to find the magnetic pole you must fly south. Suffice it to say all compasses are completely useless north of Hudson Bay and you may as well rip them from your airplane and toss them out the window. For those who like esoteric facts, the North Pole and the North Magnetic Pole lie more than a thousand miles apart with the latter leapfrogging northwestward at 25 miles a year. *Now can you begin to appreciate the problems Don was facing at Alert, since this was in the days before there was any decent navigation equipment to help him?*

They waited a couple of days for the two support ski-planes to show up, but no such luck. As a result, Don came under intense pressure to fly to the North Pole without the necessary homework that was critical to his success. Research on the pole's icepack is pretty much limited to late April and early May because of weather conditions, and if you miss that window of opportunity you must wait until the following year. Finally, he loaded the Bristol and said he'd give it a try, but only if he could keep everyone safe. One mistake and there was little chance anyone would ever see them again, let alone be able to rescue them in the icy moonscape of the polar sea.

Don left the Alert airport with the old Bristol just after midnight on May 6, 1967. He circled and flew over its runway to mark his departure time and double-check that the airplane's directional gyros were correctly set to their last known direction, then set his course for the North Pole. It was daylight because of the time of year and the midnight sun, but now there was nothing in front of him except for the wintry bleakness of the top of the world. He could only find the North Pole by using what's called dead reckoning in pilot's lingo, with all the emphasis on the "dead" part rather than the "reckoning" if he screwed up, since he was pretty much restricted to navigating by time and distance. Five-hundred-twenty miles divided by 150 miles per hour and that sort of thing, hardly an exact science because there wasn't any way of knowing if his groundspeed was correct. *Who in hell knew what the winds aloft were further north?* Despite having a veteran copilot sitting beside him and nine other men in the cargo hold, he was still the loneliest man in the world. No matter what happened, it would all rest on his shoulders.

Don and his copilot did the best they could with two other navigational devises they had on board—the astrocompass and the drift sight. The astrocompass is something like an old surveyor's transit that can be used to line up the sun, moon, or stars in a gun sight, calculate the latitude you're at, and then compute your compass direction by using the time of day, assuming your clock is absolutely correct and you have the right manuals on board so you can do the necessary astronomy. The drift sight is an instrument that lets you see wind drift left or right of your course as you fly along, giving you the chance to steer into the winds aloft to stay on a straight course across the ground, much like boating across a fast river. Since the Bristol had a cockpit that was anything but airtight, let's just say staying on course was a little like driving a speeding bus with its windows cracked open, meanwhile peering through a telescope and using bible-sized books to solve the worst mathematical problems in the world. Both men had their work cut out for them to keep from getting totally lost.

Three and half hours after liftoff they were over the North Pole just as they had hoped, but now a new problem reared its ugly head. The icepack below them looked like a jagged glacier, and as far as they could see there was nothing but snowdrifts, pressure ridges, and crevices left behind by old leads. There was no chance of landing anywhere.

The lead scientist with them had suggested that if Don couldn't find a place to land right at the pole, he should turn left and search along a course running northwestward. It was supposed the icepack in that direction would slowly drift to where the research team wanted to go, and so an airstrip anywhere along that line would meet their requirements, just as long as it wasn't too distant. Don banked the Bristol, rolled out on a diagonal heading, and started counting two miles to the minute to estimate their distance.

A few minutes later he saw something promising and descended for a look, but after buzzing the spot he saw there wasn't any way to land without wrecking the airplane. He pulled up thinking that he should head back to Alert. They had only so much fuel and all the maneuvering would likely throw off their direction gyros and they'd be lost, at least until they could reorient themselves with their astrocompass. It looked as if he was getting himself into a nasty situation by believing he could land a wheeled airplane on the sea ice.

Suddenly he saw something—a wide black lead almost a mile long—new ice from the past winter. He flew along it in one direction and then the other at 120 miles an hour and measured it for length and wind direction with a stop watch. It was three quarters of a mile long and plenty wide, but there was just one problem. A snowdrift lay right in the middle that was high enough to knock the landing gear off. He knew from years of flying around the Arctic Ocean that snowdrifts turn rock hard over time and can easily wreck an airplane. He had a tough decision to make.

He called the lead scientist up into the cockpit and powwowed with him and his copilot. Both told him they were willing for him to give it a shot, even though they stood the great chance of damaging the Bristol to the extent it couldn't fly, which meant they would die. Don decided to clip the snowdrift at landing speed on a low pass and see how hard it was, then take the chance if they damaged the airplane he could still milk it back home. It would be the biggest risk of his life.

He hit the snowdrift and it blew apart without the Bristol losing its landing gear. So far, so good, he thought. Circling, he told his copilot they would next run down their icy airstrip with the full weight of the airplane on the surface, pull up, and look for water. Otherwise, there was no way of knowing if the ice was thick enough to support twenty-plus ton.

Everything looked great after their lets-pretend landing and there was no sign of water. Don next called his engineer and loadmaster up into the cockpit. "Boys," he said, "we're going to land this time, but here's what I want you to do. The moment we slow down, start the power auger and bail out of the back door like your lives depend on it, because it surely does. Drill down to see how thick the ice is, but absolutely keep in mind that if I see any water around the landing gear and we're sinking, I'm taking off again. Drop the auger and get back on board again the moment you see the airplane move. Do you understand me?" Both nodded their heads that they did.

Don circled again, lined up on his runway, set the Bristol down, and let it roll out. He kept his right hand on both throttles and watched the ice under the left wheel for any sign of weakness. The snarl of the power auger joined the noise of the idling engines, and each second seemed like an eternity.

The ice was several feet thick, and Don Braun suddenly became a legend. His exceptional skills and knowledge as a bush pilot had paid off, and he'd accomplished something that no one had thought possible. *Who would have ever believed a bomber-sized airplane could be landed on wheels at the North Pole?* It still stands as one of the greatest achievements in aviation history, and I'm proud that he was my friend. Thank goodness, he wrote his life story, titled *The Arctic Fox*, with the help of his family, and I encourage everyone to read it. It's a great story about a very special man.

The purpose in telling Don Braun's story is to give you better insight into the polar bear's world, which, of course, is the ever-changing Arctic Ocean. It's alive, it's moving, and it constantly recycles itself. It consists of two predominate forces—new ice and old ice, one of which is the polar bear's best friend. Most people don't understand, including lots of would-be experts, that new ice means rebirth but old ice kills. Everything will die if it gets too cold and the old ice takes over, but open water and new ice let life flourish. It has to do with the sun and tiny creatures called phytoplankton.

The polar bear is at the top of the food chain, but it can't survive without the bottom, which are the microorganisms, phytoplankton that feed on the nutrient-rich freshwater that flows into the Arctic Ocean from all its tributary rivers and streams. However, phytoplankton can't grow without the sun, and what stops the sunlight? Weather that's so cold and cloudy it leaves behind ever-increasing old ice, which is thick and shuts out the life-giving light. It's critical that the icepack thaws, breaks apart, and lets everything renew itself. The sun reproduces the phytoplankton, the krill (tiny shrimp-like critters) eat it, the fish eat the krill, the seals eat the fish, and the polar bears eat the seals. It can't work any other way, nor should it, and to the extent any recent climate change has *actually* shrunk the sea ice, that's good for polar bears, not bad for the reasons I've stated.

Nowadays, it is avant-garde for most scientists to say the Arctic Ocean's icepack is melting and the polar bear will be extinct by 2050, when nothing could be further from the truth. To support their fallacious claims these supposed experts allege the polar bear is drowning because of global warming, which is completely absurd, and I challenge anyone to show me a necropsy proving *any* polar bear has drowned *anywhere* on the Arctic Ocean because of climate change. No such report exists, and you can bet if it did the national press would be publicizing it.

The myth of drowning polar bears got its start in a phony report that was given to the national press in 2005 by the U.S. Minerals Management Service, which conducts a bowhead whale survey every September off the northern coast of Alaska. In 2004, members of a government research team disingenuously suggested that four polar bears they saw floating offshore had drowned because the icepack was so far from land the poor bears couldn't find any place where they could get out of the water. What they *didn't* tell everyone was that the icepack was in the same location as it had been for almost thirty years, thus no smaller on average than it ever had been. The bottom line was they had no clue why those four bears had died. It could have been old age, fighting, or the most likely scenario—all four had been shot by Inuit hunters and escaped, only to die of their wounds later. Native Alaskans can legally hunt polar bears and often do.

The only *known* drownings of polar bears are the ones where researchers were the cause of it. For example, Canadian scientists near Pangnirtung, which is a native settlement north of Hudson Bay, darted two polars with tranquilizers in 2007 and then carelessly let both escape into the open sea where they couldn't be saved. All too often the very people who make their sanctimonious claims about the extinction of the polar bear are the ones killing them, either during their research programs or in defense of their lives because of the bad choices they make in studying animals that should be left alone. So-called experts have killed a lot more polar bears than any global warming ever has and it's time the public realizes it. There's ample reason to suspect the four polar bears north of Alaska were victims of some government study that went terribly wrong, as much as anything else.

All of this has led to the popular wisdom of polar bears being able to swim sixty miles, but always put in such a way as to suggest they are doomed because the Arctic Ocean is literally melting beneath their paws. The whole thing is bogus and only meant to brainwash the public into believing something about the High Arctic that isn't true. Polar bears could care less whether they're afoot or in the water, and they can swim a lot farther than sixty miles. Six hundred miles would be more like it, and for crying out loud, *humans* can swim sixty miles.

Two police officers killed a perfectly healthy polar bear near Skagafjordur, Iceland, on June 4, 2008, proving my point about how far they can swim without overexerting themselves. It was presumed the bear had come from Greenland, which is 200 miles away from the nearest point, although most wildlife biologists said it must have hitchhiked its way to Iceland on an iceberg. Maybe, except none were nearby, but in any event there is little room for argument about the polar bear's ability to swim a hell of a lot farther than sixty miles, which, by the way, was through the nastiest seas in the world. Let's face it, there's very little that's accurately known about the enigmatic polar bear because of the hostile environment it calls home.

Right away, there was an international outcry about the death of the bear, which, naturally, had to do with polars ostensibly being an endangered species. Iceland caught hell and deservedly so, since there was no excuse for what it had done. There's an old saying that a picture is worth a thousand words. Well, the police officers responsible for the senseless killing had someone photograph them kneeling behind their so-called *trophy* with rifles in hand, so it's clear to me the bear fell victim to a couple of guys who wanted to see themselves as heroes. Too bad they didn't realize they would come off looking like fools and place their country in the crosshairs of so much criticism. However, it didn't stop there.

Wouldn't you know just two weeks later a schoolgirl discovered another polar bear that had decided on an Icelandic vacation, however this time government officials promised everyone they would catch it alive. *What are the old sayings?* The best laid plans of mice and men go awry, and "Hullo, I'm from central government in Reykjavik and I'm here to help you." Anyway, another polar bear bit the dust, thanks to Iceland's wonderful tolerance for dangerous animals. You know the deal—*"Not in my backyard!"* It's fine for places like Churchill, Manitoba, to put up with polar bears wandering around town and native villages all across the High Arctic having to live with them, but when it comes to places like uptown Skagafjordur...well, that's an entirely different story.

Iceland's officialdom killed the second polar bear as well, using the idiotic excuse the bear had run toward the sea when they had tried tranquilizing it and so they'd had to shoot it so it couldn't swim away and endanger somebody else. *"...excuse me, which way did you say it was running?..."* I can't quite get my head wrapped around their logic, but suffice it to say we now have a pretty good idea why the polar bear might, indeed, be endangered.

Understandably, there was an even greater outcry over the slaying of the second polar bear, which actually had lots of precedent. There have been polar bears migrating to Iceland ever since humans first colonized the place, starting with the first one being discovered way back in 890. They have regularly tried setting up housekeeping on the island where there's plenty of room for them, but all have been hunted down and killed like rabid dogs. Iceland has long been known for its social welfare system and generous housing subsidies, but it's clear those benefits don't extend to wild animals.

A drumbeat then started that said the two bears had died because of global warming, which only proved lots of folks don't like being confused by the facts. First, Iceland's principal export comes from its commercial fisheries, but there was just one small problem in the spring of 2008—its fjords were so frozen the fishermen couldn't get out of their harbors. Greenland and Iceland had been hit by an exceptionally cold and long-lasting winter, which was true for the whole High Arctic from Alaska all the way east. Global warming had taken a hiatus, and so how could the Arctic Ocean be melting and causing the polar bears to jump ship when the opposite was true?

The real reason behind the two polar bears ending up dead is because Iceland is the easternmost part of their range, but its people won't let them live there. Every time the bears try, they get shot, and what's so disturbing about this is the country is now bankrupt and needs every financial opportunity it can find. Tourism accounts for almost five percent of the island's gross national product and has been growing at a ten percent annual rate, yet its government can't seem to grasp how many more tourists would visit if they could see polar bears roaming around in the wild. *"Oh, but that would be too dangerous, yah?"* Well, then explain how come Anchorage, Alaska, can live with fifty to seventy brown bears and three hundred or more black bears within its city limits with the same human population as the whole of Iceland and get along just fine with them, albeit with the exception of three recent maulings where people got a little too careless when they were bicycling and jogging near streams full of spawning salmon. There's no reason to believe Iceland can't sustain a small population of polars, and so what if it can't and they starve to death? How is that any more disastrous than what's happening to them now, and that's overlooking the fact that if they get hungry enough they will simply leave the same way they came? The Icelanders need to wake up and smell the coffee…or is it the lutefisk?

Another popular wisdom that gets passed around by the news media as scientific fact is there are only about 20,000 polar bears left in the world. Nothing could be further from the truth, inasmuch as no one has the slightest idea how many polar bears there are, which has a gargantuan home range bordered by six far-flung countries—Alaska (United States), Canada, Greenland (Denmark), Iceland, Norway, and Russia, none of which get along particularly well or are willingly to share any information. On top of this is the nasty little dispute that most people don't know about between Canada, Russia, and the United States over who *really* owns the High Arctic and its mythical "Open Polar Sea," which many of the world's scientists once again think exists… you just can't quite sail there yet, at least not without a nuclear-powered icebreaker.

My old friend, Don Braun, comes to mind once again, since he returned to the North Pole in 1969 with the same scientists, who were determined to learn more about the top of the world. One of the first things they did was drill through the ice to see what they could find, and much to their amazement a seal popped up in one their holes. Don said he was a little incredulous the research team seemed so surprised that seals were living at the pole after they'd already seen polar bear and arctic fox tracks nearby. It was all part of the ecological system that makes up the sea ice as far as Don was concerned.

The point I'm making is the Arctic Ocean is so vast and mysterious it's virtually impossible to calculate the number of polar bears that live on its pack ice. Even today with all our GPS-(global positioning system) equipped airplanes and helicopters, we still can't safely fly in the High Arctic for most of the year because of its horrendous weather and sheer distances where there are no airports or fuel. Money can't buy a helicopter that can fly to the North Pole and back since none carry enough fuel to make the round trip, let alone get there in the first place. Some airplanes can, but it stretches their range and leaves no time at all to fly grids to count how many polar bears live below, not to mention they are notoriously hard to spot against the snow anyway. The only way you can reliably find them is to locate their tracks first and chase them down, which is hardly any way to conduct a scientific survey.

I have never doubted that Canada has 20,000 polar bears all on its own, let alone how many more live above Russia and the rest of the world. There are 4,500 living around Hudson Bay by itself according to the Canadian Wildlife Service, and that's only a small part of the map when you compare its size to the entire Arctic Ocean. There's every reason to believe 50,000 or more polar bears are spread across the top of the world, but that doesn't fit what most experts believe and so we'll never know the truth, leastwise not in my lifetime.

Interestingly, the Inuit in the western Hudson Bay region, which is now part of what's called Nunavut, believe there are more polar bears than ever and they want to increase the numbers they harvest through big-game guiding and subsistence hunting. The Canadian Wildlife Service disagrees, claiming there are less bears because of thinning sea ice and that all hunting should be significantly cut, if not stopped altogether. This has upset the Inuit because they say they're the ones having to live with the bears, they're being attacked more often, and Canada's scientific studies are wrong, let alone that their traditional knowledge and wisdom is being ignored for the sake of computer modeling by a bunch of pinheads who have never set foot on the pack ice (something that was said to me by someone in the Inuit community who wishes to remain anonymous).

Something else that's fanning the flames of this bitter argument that most folks don't know about is the Inuit earn as much as $50,000 for every sportsman they take out polar bear hunting, which has never set well with the pencil pushers and politicians in Ottawa, let alone the rest of the world. *Does Marie Antoinette's "let them eat cake" ring a bell?* Sadly, that has a lot more to do with it than meets the eye, and there are a good many people in high places who would much rather see the Inuit go extinct than the polar bear. Stay tuned because this nasty fight is far from over, and there are lots of things hanging in the balance.

The winter of 2007 through 2008 added a new wrinkle to the polar bear's fortunes and misfortunes as well, since it was one of those old-fashioned winters with lots of snow and plenty of subzero temperatures. Anchorage, Alaska, for example, was left with one of its coldest years on record and fresh snow on its neighboring mountains in July, and in nearby Prince William Sound, the site of the infamous Exxon Valdez oil spill, there was still snow at sea level in midsummer, which was unheard of before. Global warming had gotten the hiccups.

Meanwhile, the climate-change crowd begrudgingly admitted the Arctic Ocean had once again frozen to its old-time dimensions, except now it was with the wrong kind of ice. *The wrong kind of ice!* I didn't quite know what to think when I heard that one, since I've already said that polar bears can only survive and prosper if there's sunlight, open water, phytoplankton, new ice, etcetera. But never fear, because before I could take a second breath, the scientists were quickly saying the icepack had shrunk by fifty percent during the summer and they were right about global warming after all. I didn't know what to say, since the High Arctic's sea ice has always shrunken by about half in the summertime, which is why Henry Hudson and Sir John Franklin got themselves and their sailors into so much trouble so long ago searching for the Northwest Passage, let alone about a million other explorers later on. The English could never get it in their heads the High Arctic couldn't care less what mere mortals think, and I suspect the same thing holds true today. No one has figured out how to conquer the Arctic Ocean yet, but now it seems lots of people believe they can do it with their computers. I'm afraid they will leave nothing behind but for their bones just like so many other so-called experts have in the past. The top of the world is timeless.

I've flown the Bermuda Triangle and looked down at its dark waters and remembered all its faceless victims, and I've flown over the Gulf of Mexico when it was so black you could cut the night with a knife. I've seen the Bering Sea and North Pacific when long rolling waves were bursting into foaming seawater flying on the wind. I've crossed Cook Inlet in a helicopter at a hundred feet and hopped the width of Lake Michigan a dozen times, but nothing has stuck in my mind more than the sea ice I've seen covering Hudson Bay off Churchill, Manitoba, farther north at Rankin Inlet, and at Chantrey Inlet, which is south of King William Island. The pack ice between Nome, Alaska, and the village of Savoonga on St. Lawrence Island left even more of an impression on me, maybe because I could see Siberia in the distance. Only then did I begin to understand the infinity of the sea ice as opposed to the insignificance of human beings. We don't matter much in the scheme of things.

It never occurred to me for most of my life that anyone would ever need to worry about the polar bear, let alone being attacked by one, and that it would become the poster child in a geopolitical fight over something as unpredictable and poorly understood as the weather. Almost no one visited the High Arctic except for a few floatplane pilots like me, and the Inuit and Swampy Cree knew how to take care of themselves when it came to bears. Separation was the key to their safety, or they simply killed any bear that became a threat to them. As far as any travelers were concerned, something that an old Canadian Mountie told me was the law of the land, "Son, you better have claw marks on you if you shoot a polar bear." That seemed perfectly clear to me.

I never slept in a tent when I was in polar bear country, choosing to sleep in my airplane since I would be easily warned of an attack, not to mention hazardous changes in the weather. The High Arctic is mostly barren, so it wasn't a problem to spot one in the distance, especially under the midnight sun. It wasn't as if one could sneak up on you if you were in the open and it wasn't wintertime. Otherwise, I kept my bear gun handy and didn't make stupid choices regarding where I was fishing and camping. There was no bear spray back then, and usually the wind was blowing so hard it wouldn't have worked anyway. High winds were a constant threat.

Nowadays, things have changed. Women are floating down the remote Back River into Chantrey Inlet; a young man was blogging about kayaking from York Factory to Port Nelson, which would be almost as suicidal as one could get given the hurricane-force winds, tidal races, and polar bears that frequent the bottom of Hudson Bay; and middle-aged couples are canoeing down the Hayes River into York Factory where the Canadian government has prohibited camping because of the polar bear population. Wherever one turns, tourists are traveling to such places as Churchill for their once-in-a-lifetime trip to see the Arctic and its bears, which was almost unheard of not so many years ago. Alaska and Canada have now become playgrounds for people who don't even know how to start a campfire, let alone survive a bear attack.

Even the Inuit are having problems with the polars. Not long ago a young hunting guide who was sleeping in his tent was attacked by a midsized polar. The Northern News Services, which serves the High Arctic, reported that Kootoo Shaw saw the bear rip into his tent and immediately ran for his life. Except that he tripped and the bear started tearing him to shreds, leaving him with broken ribs, almost scalped, and with deep wounds all over his back. The Americans he was guiding on Baffin Island luckily were able to kill the bear just in time to save his life, but not from the three hundred staples it took to put his hair back on again, let alone all the other sutures it took to treat him. Snopes.com has carried news and colored pictures of the attack as well, which vividly show how dangerous polar bears can be. People simply don't recognize they see humans as easy prey and often attack without warning. Never let your guard down if you want to stay alive.

A Native-Alaskan living in Fort Yukon can attest to that. He came within a few feet of getting pounced on by a polar bear in the last place in the world he expected to see one. The *Fairbanks Daily News-Miner* reported on March 28, 2008, that Zeb Cadzow shot a female polar at pointblank range when it attacked him on the Porcupine River not far from town. All 900 townspeople were stunned when they heard the news, let alone the usual rope line of bear experts. Fort Yukon is almost three hundred miles from the Beaufort Sea, but that's as a crow flies. This bear had obviously traveled a lot farther, including crossing the 8,000-foot Brooks Range in the dead of winter. Nonetheless, it was in prime condition and clearly had been eating well.

One of the townspeople had spotted a white bear feeding on skinned lynx carcasses that a fur trapper had thrown into a pile beside his cabin. The bear had run off and no one believed Peter

John when he said it certainly looked white to him. Everyone figured it must be a grizzly that was covered with frost and snow, or maybe it was an albino of some sort. Regardless, some hunters followed its tracks because springtime bears, particularly the tundra grizzly that's found in this part of Alaska, are notorious for being hotheaded, hungry, and not at all above killing and eating school kids and sled dogs. Everyone wanted the threat removed as soon as possible.

Cadzow tracked the bear onto a brushy island in the middle of the nearby Porcupine River, only to find himself being attacked by a polar bear that had been waiting in ambush for him. Fortunately, he had a semiautomatic rifle and since he didn't have time to aim, just started pulling the trigger. Lucky for him, he was a good snapshot or he'd now be sleeping with his ancestors, one of whom was a 102-year-old woman who had just passed away. The Fort Yukon people said she must have had powerful medicine to bring a polar bear to them, which made just as much sense as anything the wildlife biologists had to say, since none of them could explain why a polar would be living so far inland. For some odd reason, they seem to forget the polar bear is the ultimate survivalist and can live almost anywhere it wants.

They are great travelers and have been reported on Kodiak Island, along the Kamchatka Peninsula and the Kuril Islands on the Sea of Okhotsk, which isn't far from Japan, and also in Norway. Iceland, of course, is a regular stop for them as I've said before, and they are commonly seen on James Bay, which reaches into southern Canada. Especially nowadays, people are being sold on the idea polar bears can't live without sea ice, but that isn't true at all. As with all bears, they will subsist on whatever is available. Waterfowl and their eggs, newborn chicks, seaweeds, berries, musk-ox, caribou and reindeer, walrus, whales, other bears, and in the case of most Arctic villages, garbage from their dumps—it's all on their bill of fare. Bears will be bears and polars are no exception. So keep your distance, the wind in your favor, and yourself well hidden at all times.

Finally, the great white bear that I saw at Eskimo Point one summer will always be etched into my mind, and I will take that image to my grave. I was flying up to Rankin Inlet on a clear day and this big polar was spread-eagled on a hilltop overlooking Hudson Bay. He was looking out to sea but then looked up at me, and I'll never forget how lucky that made me feel. There is nothing better than seeing Mother Nature at her finest, and I was reminded of the Inuit legend that says, "In the beginning, the raven made the world. He was a god and a bird with a human inside." Suddenly, life seemed so clear to me because of the wisdom of an earlier civilization, and I felt just like the raven. It was one of my best days.

DOUBLE STANDARD

ON JUNE 18, 2007, the *Deseret News* and *The Salt Lake Tribune*
in Salt Lake City, Utah, both reported the death of 11-year-
old Sam Ives, ripped from the family tent he was sleeping in
with his parents and little brother the night before. His family had been awakened when he'd suddenly shrieked that he
was being dragged in his sleeping bag through a hole that had
been slashed in the tent's sidewall. At first, it was thought that
someone had used a knife or razorblade because the cut was
so clean, but it wouldn't take long to learn the boy had died a
much more horrible death than at the hands of some perverted
murderer. This prowler was more like an ogre.

Sam's stepfather had driven the family into the American
Fork Canyon, a popular outdoor spot thirty miles southeast of
Salt Lake, to celebrate Father's Day in a new tent Sam had bought
for their special holiday. They set up their campsite a mile or so
past the Timpooneke Campground in the Uinta National Forest,
but near where others were camping as well. On Sunday night
they went to sleep only to be awakened by Sam's bloodcurdling
screams in the pitch dark.

His stepfather instantly started searching for him but didn't have a flashlight, so he jumped into his car and raced to the Timpooneke caretaker's house trailer and beat on his door looking for help. The caretaker drove to a payphone and alerted law enforcement to the missing boy. A couple of hours later, the Utah County sheriff's office said that searchers had found Sam's body a quarter mile away from the campsite, or at least what was left of him. It was clear the attack had been made by a predatory bear.

The next day, Utah wildlife officers tracked the bear with more than two dozen dogs, and then after the embarrassment of wounding it and having to hunt for it for several more hours, they finally killed the good-sized black and had a necropsy performed to prove it was the same one that had preyed on Sam. The report came back positive and Utah had its first recorded fatal bear attack, but little did everybody know things wouldn't stop there.

Right away, reporters from both newspapers began questioning the appropriate officials about the details of the attack, intent on learning how such a tragedy could have taken place. As expected, the director of the Utah Division of Wildlife, a fellow named Jim Karpowitz, was one of the first to be interviewed. His answers were unsurprising, since I swear that federal and state bureaucrats somewhere in the past have sent talking points back and forth so they can say identical things no matter where the bear predation occurs. "Bears are short of food when it's hot and dry like this," he told a newspaper reporter. Contradicting that, however, was the bear wasn't undernourished and looked in fine shape for the time of year, and so I'm reminded of 93-year-old Adelia Maestas Trujillo's death in New Mexico, whom I wrote about early on. "The bears are hungry," the authorities had explained, "because all the acorns and berries have been destroyed by spring frosts and a summer drought." *What is it about people in official positions that stop them from acknowledging that bears are dangerous predators and must be managed accordingly?*

It didn't stop there, and another interview by a reporter for the *Deseret News* literally took my breath away. A well-known bear expert named Barrie K. Gilbert, who had spent twenty-seven years at Utah State University as a behavior ecologist studying them, was quizzed about the predation in the American Fork Canyon. The first thing he said was where we were in full agreement, but later on he completely lost me. "...people should be careful around bears because they're big and dangerous," he said from his retirement home in Ontario, Canada. That much is true and no one could have said it any better, but what he said afterward were the remarks that upset me, especially since he survived a grizzly mauling once upon a time. "One possibility," he said, "is the bear might have heard something inside the tent that sounded like a mouse and pounced on it." Then he added later on, "They're almost cunning." Assuming the reporter didn't get his statements wrong, which I won't argue happens way too often, I was left shaking my head. *'...sounded like a mouse?'*

Let's get some facts straight. First, that black bear knew *exactly* what it was doing, and to suppose it had mistaken Sam for a mouse is preposterous to the point of being silly. Bears have noses so sharp they can distinguish anything they want to the nth degree, and they never pounce on anything without being fully aware of what they are doing. Secondly, bears have night vision that's better than any Green Beret equipped with the best night goggles money can buy. That black could see Sam's tent clearly and knew precisely where he was sleeping because of his scent. As far as hearing is concerned, there should be no question it could hear every last sound in the tent, but that just helped it zero in on its prey. Sam was just the right size and wouldn't put up much of a fight. Finally, to believe bears "are almost cunning" is naivety of the most unforgivable kind, particularly for someone who has studied bears for so long. The words bears and cunning are like two peas in a pod, and you must never forget how sneaky and smart they are, not if you want to stay alive.

It didn't take long for Sam's parents to learn that authorities had been warned earlier in the day that a black bear had been raiding coolers and taken a swipe at another small boy inside a tent, but had failed to do anything about it, other than pay lip service to the fact they might have to euthanize the bear when they got around to it. Understandably, the Ives were mad as hell and hired a lawyer who sued both the National Forest Service and the Utah Division of Wildlife for their combined negligence.

According to *The Salt Lake Tribune* on November 19, 2008, Assistant U.S. Attorney Amy Oliver argued in court there was no requirement for federal agencies to post warnings or close campgrounds because bears were attacking people. *A young boy gets killed and eaten and this is what we get for our tax dollars?* Without a doubt, this proves how morally bankrupt our public servants have become and, frankly, I don't know how a lot them get up in the morning and look in the mirror.

Now let's turn everything around and imagine what would have happened if the Ives had let their campfire get away and start a forest fire that cost a firefighter his or her life or their Rottweiler, presuming they owned one, had attacked and killed a ranger? The Forest Service would have sued them for every last thing they owned and couldn't have cared less if their two boys would starve to death because of the lawsuit. Talk about a double standard, this one really fries me.

The precedent for the Ives lawsuit was a 1996 bear attack reported by the *Arizona Daily Star*, which is Tucson's main newspaper. A teenage girl named Anna Knochel was taking part in a 4-H camping trip on Mount Lemmon, a national forest northeast of the city, when a black bear snuck into her tent, dragged her out, and for all practical purposes started eating her before she was dead. Her screams saved her because they brought someone on the run to rescue her, but she was left with terrible wounds, flesh missing from one leg, and paralysis. Her parents learned the National Forest Service and State of Arizona had been well aware of this particular bear since it had just injured a Girl Scout Brownie and they had done nothing more than relocate it nine miles away, which accomplished nothing at all because it came right back. Her parents sued Arizona, the Forest Service, and the 4-H Club for 15 million dollars, which got them a settlement of 2.5 million from the state alone.

On August 11, 2008, the Knoxville, Tennessee, *News Sentinel* reported a similar attack on an 8-year-old boy. John Pala and his two boys had flown from Florida to spend a few days in the Great Smoky Mountains National Park, which is easily accessed from Gatlinburg off Cherokee Orchard Road. On the evening of their arrival, they bought Kentucky Fried Chicken, drove their rental car to the head of the Rainbow Falls trail, and after locking their leftovers in the car, started to do some exploring before it got dark. They walked a short ways and came to a split-log bridge that spanned a creek. John and his oldest son, 10-year-old Alex, started across, but little Evan ran down to play in the water. His father told him to come back and not get his feet wet, so he turned around, but then was flattened from behind by a small black bear. Understandably, he screamed for help at the top of his lungs.

His dad leapt into action, pulled the bear off of him, and yelled for both kids to run for the car. Both took off, but then Evan tripped and the bear pounced on him again, ripping at him like a buzz saw. Again, Pala grabbed the bear and yanked it off his boy, except this time he positioned himself so it couldn't attack again. Alex and he threw sticks and stones as hard as they could while shuffling backward, then ran for their lives. Another family in the parking lot saw them racing back all bloody and bruised and called an ambulance to rush them to a hospital where Evan was patched together again. Thankfully, his wounds weren't life-threatening and his dad was only clawed up a little, although all three decided they'd had enough of the Smoky Mountains for the time being. Pala had run so hard he'd lost his shoes and his toes looked as if someone had taken a weedwacker after them.

Park rangers found the bear later on, it attacked them as well, so they shot it and sent the carcass to the University of Tennessee for a necropsy. It was a teenager weighing less than one hundred pounds, which I wrote earlier is oftentimes the most dangerous bear of all. Now think of the situation if Pala had been carrying a hefty walking stick, since that bear would have been punished severely. In addition, please understand that bear spray wouldn't have worked because Evan would have gotten a bigger dose than the bear.

The reason I've told you the true stories of the three children is to drive home the point where the greatest danger lies and what can be done about it, especially nowadays when people know a lot more about BlackBerries than black bears. As I said before, they present the biggest problem because of their exceptional intelligence, vast range, and sheer numbers, especially as it comes to our state and national parks where they are never hunted. They have essentially lost their fear of humans in the past fifty years or so, or it's been bred out of them if you want to look at it like that. Thus, with our campgrounds getting older and seeing more use, many have become bear magnets because they have become likely food sources that smell just like hamburgers, hotdogs, and humans. In the instance of Anna Knochel, it was learned that people were feeding bears nearby, so was it any wonder one attacked her? But this simply illustrates the problems we face, since the managers of our parks and campgrounds are failing us by not implementing well thought-out wildlife management. It's only after someone gets seriously hurt or killed that any steps are taken, which then inevitably results in a dead bear when everything could have been prevented in the first place. It's certainly not too much to ask that our federal and state employees take a more proactive and smarter approach to bear management, see the public is fully educated about the dangers they present, and that every man, woman, and child is sufficiently warned when our recreational areas are threatened by them. Think of it this way, what would our government employees do if a serial killer were on the loose in our parks? Of course, you know the answer.

The most important thing is for everyone to stop believing that bears are bedwetting pacifists that only kill to keep from starving to death. Nothing could be further from the truth, since all are clever hunters and meat and fish are their primary food sources whenever either is available to them. For the last twenty or thirty years, bear experts have portrayed them as peace lovers that would walk right past a baby deer provided there's enough acorns or berries for them to eat. That's complete nonsense, and bears are every bit as skilled at hunting as the mountain lion or the wolf, with the advantage of being considerably bigger and smarter. In fact, it's been observed in Alaska and our western states that black bears and grizzlies often kill more caribou, elk, and moose calves than wolves do because they are such proficient predators. Never underestimate how adept bears are when it comes to hunting, and it's very hard to escape them once they've set their sights on something.

Another good example of what's taking place nowadays is the grizzly attack the *Anchorage Daily News* wrote about on August 29, 2008. Jo Ann Staples of Kentucky came within an eyelash of losing her life, and but for her kicking and screaming, along with the courage of her wilderness guides, she would be singing with the angels. Her story speaks volumes about the do's and don'ts when it comes to camping in grizzly country.

She was on an all-women adventure trip in the Brooks Range almost a thousand miles north of Anchorage when the attack occurred. After a week of watching migrating caribou in the Gates of the Arctic National Park, she had gotten up early to pack her things for a bush flight back to civilization. It was still dark out so she was using a headlamp to see in her tent, but then all hell broke loose. An explosion of teeth and claws ripped into her from outside, leaving her with no hope but to fight for her life. She started hitting, kicking, and screaming as hard as she could, despite being tangled in torn polyester.

Anne Dellenbaugh, owner of the guiding business named "Her Wilderness Song" and assistant guide, Sharon Sandstrum, heard Staples' cries and flew to her rescue. Dellenbaugh charged at the bear while banging a pot and pan, followed by Sandstrum, who was carrying their bear spray. The bear stopped its attack, stood up, dropped back down, and walked toward them. They test-fired the pepper spray, but not at the bear for some inexplicable reason, although the hissing sound and orange mist drove it away nonetheless. They ran, cut Staples free of her tent, and used a satellite telephone to call Coyote Air out of Coldfoot, which is a truck stop along the Dalton Highway, or what is known by Alaskans as the "Haul Road," since it's the gravel road that services the oil fields at Prudhoe Bay. True to the bush operators of Alaska, Coyote was there in a flash, landed on a gravel bar on a nearby river, and got her back into Coldfoot for a medevac flight into Fairbanks in time to save her life, although her wounds were serious and would take a long time to heal.

The Gates of the Arctic National Park superintendent, Greg Dudgeon, told the *Daily News* the same things we've heard countless times before—the women's camp was clean, their food was stored in bear-proof containers in a separate tent a safe distance away, and attacks on tents with people inside are so rare that scientists can't even guess as to what triggers them. And he felt this attack was particularly strange because the grizzly had raided the food tent first and tried breaking into the food containers, but had failed. After that, it had stalked Staples for some unknown reason. ...Once again, I'm disturbed by what was simply overlooked in all this. *How about that bears have acute noses that can smell things from great distances, they're opportunistic hunters, and they were given teeth and claws to kill and eat other living things?*

For the umpteenth time, just because you keep a tidy camp and store your food in bear-proof containers doesn't mean a bear can't smell everything from miles away under the right weather conditions. Actually, one could make a half-decent argument that it might have been better if Dellenbaugh would have let the damn bear have the food with the hope it would eat its fill and leave everyone alone. Bears aren't picky eaters, they gulp down tinfoil and plastic wrappers without hesitation, so it doesn't take long for them to get a bellyache and decide it's time to sleep it off. The problem you have, though, is they will come right back as soon as they wake up and they never want to take no for an answer the second time around, which means you must kill them. Not a good situation at all.

The bear that attacked Staples was pissed off because it couldn't break into the food containers, and so it was in an ugly mood when it first spotted her headlamp come on and start bobbing around in her tent. *Probably looked just like a roadside diner with a flashing neon sign, and I doubt there's a bear in the world that wouldn't sneak up for a better look.* It was hopping mad, certain it was starving now that it had been aggravated to no end, and all of a sudden there's warm-blooded prey right in front of its nose. For crying out loud, under the circumstances, why would anyone wonder why it had attacked, it was only doing what bears are meant to do. Would anyone wonder why killer bees sting or rattlesnakes bite?

Camping in grizzly country isn't for the fainthearted and sensible precautions must be taken. The biggest quandary is that you usually don't know there's a bear problem until it's too late, as Staples and her guides found out. Frankly, I wouldn't trek in the Gates of the Arctic National Park without posting a guard at night or using some kind of protection device to wake me in time to defend myself. The tundra grizzlies in that part of Alaska are simply too dangerous for anyone to assume he or she is safe from an attack. They have little fear of humans, there's not much for them to eat, and predation is a big part of their lives. It's plan ahead or pay the price in that part of the North.

The attacks on Ives, Knochel, Pala, and Staples have a common theme, right along with all the others I've written about throughout this book: people are getting attacked and sometimes eaten because of the unforgivable lack of knowledge about bears and what it takes to protect oneself against them. People are letting themselves get into situations where they are dangerously exposed—sometimes because they have no idea there are any bears around, sometimes because they think bears aren't dangerous, and sometimes because they get way too careless. This is complicated by the fact that those who are in management positions, such as directors of state wildlife divisions and national park superintendents, have let everyone down with a lack of professionalism, either because of ignorance about bears, their environmental agendas, or poor job performances, if not all three. We need change.

Consequently, I have hit hard at bear experts, bureaucrats, park superintendents, and others throughout this book, often using irony and sarcasm to make my point. I have vented my frustration at individuals who have failed to save others from being mauled or killed simply because they want everyone to believe that bears pose little threat to humans, their diets consists of innocuous things, and in any case they're nearing extinction and must be saved at all costs. None of that is true, and it never serves anyone's purpose to manage wildlife by false pretenses, nor is it helpful to mislead people about the largest and smartest predators on earth. For thousands of years, native peoples saw them for what they were, worshipped them as deities, and stayed away from them. Seems to me they had it right.

On the flip side of my criticism of those in high places is the fact that North America's bear populations are healthy and in some instances, even increasing. So in that sense I'm wrong in suggesting that everyone in the bear business doesn't know what they're doing. The individuals who determine the hunting seasons in Alaska, Canada, and the forty-eight contiguous states have done a good job in managing our different species of bears, especially when you realize that it's an almost impossible, thankless task. Bear viewing, subsistence hunting, sport hunting, euthanization, self-defense, cannibalism, too many in one place and not enough in another—the folks who make all the final decisions on the bear's fate have done well despite catching hell from all sides. I wouldn't want their job because you can't win and somebody's bound to call you dirty names.

In any event, I feel it's important to review the things I've written about regarding protecting yourself when you're visiting bear country, whether it's in the Voyageurs National Park in Northern Minnesota where there are only blacks, Montana or Idaho where you never know when you might run into a grizzly sow with cubs, Alaska where a brown might weigh 1,500 pounds, or the High Arctic where you might be stalked by a polar bear. It makes no difference where you are, the following general guidelines will apply.

Take Inventory of Yourself

Are you the ballerina-type from the big city or a veteran outdoorsman who can sleep under a canoe for days on end and think you're in seventh heaven? Your physical size, strength, and courage all play critical roles in your ability to survive a dangerous confrontation with a bear. A petite woman with little kids is just asking for trouble if she's off by herself in bear country, whereas an Alaskan or Canadian hunting guide can wander around the same place with nothing more than a knife and some matches and stay relatively safe.

The difference? Once again and with great fear of being so repetitious, bears can smell things better than bloodhounds and have an extraordinary sixth-sense to back it up. It's one thing for them to come across someone who freaks out and drops all of his or her defenses the moment he or she feels threatened and another to attack someone who looks like a middle linebacker for the New York Giants and just happens to be carrying a club the size of a fencepost, right along with the disposition to use it. Bears aren't dumb, always size up their prey, and plan accordingly, even though they might only have a split-second to do it. Consequently, rate yourself on a scale of one to ten and organize your outdoor adventures accordingly, and for God's sake, be realistic and leave your fat head at home.

Part of your inventory should include the number, sex, physical size, and grit of your friends as well. It's one thing to visit bear country all alone and quite another if there are six or seven of you, and as I've said before, bears hate being outnumbered and think in the terms of wolf packs. One of the most revealing wildlife photographs I've ever seen is of an Alaskan grizzly surrounded by a dozen wolves. Despite that bear being much larger and a great deal stronger than any one of those wolves, or any two for that matter, the absolute fear on its face is palpable. There's an important message there for everyone, so think about what it means.

Choose Your Weapon

Once you've taken inventory of yourself and the people who will be accompanying you, then you can decide on the defensive weapons you should carry. Children mean one thing and a half-dozen triathletes mean quite another. Black bears in particular like to zero in on kids, so you must take that into consideration when you're visiting our state and national parks that have big populations of them. Just a little preparation goes a long way.

Binoculars, policeman's flashlights, heavy-duty walking sticks, and canisters of bear spray are, of course, the basics you should carry along, but there are other things to add to your equipment as well, depending on the kind of bear country you're visiting. Everything from a bear rifle to a machete should be considered, partly for survival reasons and partly for defense. Flare guns have proved to be effective as bear deterrents, and I've also written about stun guns and my PackAlarm. Err on the side of caution, rather than cop an attitude that nothing will ever hurt you, and don't forget your belt knife and waterproof matches either. You will be awfully glad to have them along if you tip over in a canoe or get flipped upside down in a floatplane.

Silence is Golden

Whoever came up with the bright idea of wearing tinkling bells and hooting and hollering as you trek through bear country ought to be taken out and horsewhipped, if for no other reason than I've had my wilderness experiences ruined too many times by the idiocy of people shouting in full chorus while they're passing through the backcountry. I'm not out there to see every bird, deer, wolf, fox, caribou, and whatever else spooked clean out of the country, and besides there's not one shred of evidence or any research that says that noisemaking effectively scares predatory bears in the least. In fact, there's every reason to worry that it makes them curious because they're the dominate species, which isn't the smartest thing to do. And besides, on most days the wind is so strong the trees, brush, and water are whipped into such frenzy that bears can't hear anything until you almost step on them anyway. Go to a football game if you want to wear little bells and scream your head off and stop spoiling the reason I'm out in the wilds.

Modern man has gotten along just fine with everything from the saber-toothed cat to the present-day bear for about 170,000 years, but then suddenly someone came up with the foolishness in the last part of the twentieth century that we should stop using the stealthy survival skills we had perfected for millennia and resort to becoming noisy monkeys too afraid to come out of the trees. I don't get it, and it strikes me that it should be obvious to everybody that if we could survive with primitive weapons for so long, then we should use the same wilderness bushcraft today with the added help of our high-tech gear. Binoculars, bear spray, firearms—we have effective tools, and so there's no excuse for spoiling the outdoors with silly shouting. Stay at home if you're that scared of bears.

Bears are creatures of habit, the same as us, and you can predict where you might run into them and avoid those areas or at least stay on high alert. In the springtime, they're eating sedges and prowling the calving grounds for newborn deer, elk, moose, and caribou. Later in the summer, they're hunting, fishing, and eating insects they find under rocks along rivers, lakeshores, and in mountain passes. Toward fall, they're hanging around berry patches and watching for targets of opportunity, since this is when they must pile on the weight. The experts say they're omnivorous, which is true as far as that goes, but never forget all bears will kill and eat another animal species, including man, whenever they get the chance. There is a God-given reason why they have fangs and claws and the ferocity to use them.

Separation is the key to bear safety as I've written before, and that comes about because of outdoor skills. Camouflage clothing, keeping to the high ground, stopping, looking, and listening, judicious use of binoculars, keeping track of the wind, and cautiously moving from one place to another are the things that will keep you safe in the outdoors, the same skills that ancient people used back to Neanderthal times. Attend a bowhunting school, study animal tracks and their scat, and practice sneaking up on deer to learn the intricacies of expert bushcraft, and you will be amazed at how well stealth works when it comes to avoiding bears. If it was good enough for our ancestors, it's certainly good enough for us.

First Aid

I always carried a first aid kit when I visited isolated places. Alaska, Canada, and many other wild areas are such that once you reach your destination, especially by airplane or helicopter, you're stuck there until the pilot can come back for you, meaning if he or she is delayed by bad weather or, God forbid, killed in a crash on the way out, you might be stranded for a very long time. My first aid kit consisted of the essentials that would keep someone alive for several days, having been put together by a doctor friend of mine. It wasn't cheap to buy, but it was remarkably helpful from time to time and brought me great peace of mind on some of my riskier trips. The High Arctic, in particular, is an unforgiving place and several days can pass before someone can rescue you. Nitroglycerin tablets, pain pills, penicillin and antibiotics—my kit was sophisticated enough to keep someone alive under some pretty rough circumstances.

In addition to my first aid kit, I always carried an emergency location transmitter. These little radios signal your exact position to satellites that in turn alert search and rescue to your emergency. Since 2003, it has become legal for individuals to carry personal locator beacons that had been restricted to aircraft and boats for the longest time, thanks to our government's dubious policy and foresight. Why the bureaucrats didn't want the general public to be safe is beyond me, but nevertheless you can now buy a pocket-sized radio that could very well save your life. They're expensive, since you will spend almost $700, but they will last a lifetime and are worth their weight in gold if you are injured in the middle of nowhere. Just imagine what your chances are if you are mauled by a grizzly in the Yukon Territory and your bush pilot isn't due back for several days. Without first aid and a personal locator beacon, your chances of survival are slim to none.

Finally, I have been deliberately critical of supposed experts, law enforcement people, and state and federal officials who always become the focal point when someone is killed and eaten by a bear. Too often, they have let us down with their ineffectiveness, questionable agendas, and disturbing lack of knowledge when it comes to predatory bears, in particular the ubiquitous black. Children are preyed upon and they make excuses, rather than establish professional management programs that benefit everyone and protect our natural resources as well. Unbeknownst to the public, most bears now meet their fate by the "shoot, shovel, and shut up" process, especially in grizzly country. We must do better, so if this book saves even one person's life, along with a bear's, I've done my job.

BIBLIOGRAPHY

Books

Ambrose, Stephen. *Undaunted Courage*. New York: Simon & Schuster, 2005.

Bennett, Bo. *Rods & Wings*. Anchorage: Publication Consultants, 2000.

Franklin, John. *Narrative of a Journey to the Shores of the Polar Sea in the Years of 1819–20*. London: John Murray, 1824.

Jans, Nick. *The Grizzly Maze*. New York: Penguin Group, 2006.

Kaniut, Larry. *Alaska Bear Tales*. Portland: Alaska Northwest Books, 1983.

Moulton, Gary, Editor. *The Journals of the Lewis & Clark Expedition*. Lincoln: University of Nebraska Press, 1988.

Warren, John. *The Arctic Fox: Bush Pilot of the North Country*. Lincoln: IUniverse, 2000.

Wright, Gerald. *Wrangell-Saint Elias International Wilderness*. Anchorage: Alaska Geographic Society, 1981.

Newspapers

Medred, Craig. "Wildlife author killed, eaten by bears he loved." *Anchorage Daily News,* October 8, 2003.

Medred, Craig. "Treadwell: 'Get out here. I'm getting killed.'" *Anchorage Daily News,* October 9, 2003.

Bennet, Joel. "Treadwell cared for future of bears." *Anchorage Daily News,* October 16, 2003.

Medred, Craig. "Treadwell lived life in vastly different worlds." *Anchorage Daily News,* October 25, 2003.

Medred, Craig. "Park Service says mauling not at night." *Anchorage Daily News,* January 6, 2004.

Stringham, Stephen. "Treadwell's killer had to be killed." *Anchorage Daily News,* March 6, 2004.

Medred, Craig. "Deadly ending." *Anchorage Daily News,* March 28, 2004.

Medred, Craig. "Woman who died with 'bear guru' was duped." *Anchorage Daily News,* January 16, 2005.

Medred, Craig. "Authors' lies do readers no favors." *Anchorage Daily News,* February 5, 2005.

Ruskin, Liz. "Morbid curiosity the bait of Treadwell film 'Grizzly Man.'" *Anchorage Daily News,* August 19, 2005.

Johnson, Scott. "It's not the bears acting unnaturally." *Anchorage Daily News,* August 26, 2005.

Bryson, George. "Author set out to discover the real Timothy Treadwell." *Anchorage Daily News,* September 26, 2005.

Kobak, Ed. "Treadwell invited others to see bears." *Anchorage Daily News*, October 19, 2005.

Potempa, Ann. "Coroner draws national attention." *Anchorage Daily News*, December 11, 2005.

Simpson, Sherry. "A Short, Happy Life." *Anchorage Daily News*, October 13, 1996.

Bryson, George. "The Last Days of Michio Hoshino." *Anchorage Daily News*, October 13, 1996.

Aho, Karen. "Man dies after mauling." *Anchorage Daily News*, April 17, 2007.

Holland, Megan. "Three shots end fierce mauling of hunter." *Anchorage Daily News*, April 18, 2007.

Medred, Craig. "Bear attack leaves one dead, another hurt." *Anchorage Daily News*, April 18, 2007.

Miller, Andrew. "Mine workers see bears fight to the death." *Anchorage Daily News (The Sitka Daily Sentinel)*, July 21, 2006.

Medred, Craig. "Guide saved woman during bear attack." *Anchorage Daily News*, August 29, 2008.

Medred, Craig. "Retiree welcomes neighborhood bears." *Anchorage Daily News*, April 15, 2007.

Medred, Craig. "Bear-ly believable." *Anchorage Daily News*, January 18, 2008.

Garner, Joe. "Bear Kills 93 Year-Old New Mexico Woman." *Scripps Howard News Service*, August 21, 2001.

Nash, Al and Vallie, Stacy. "Nature Photographer Identified as Yellowstone Bear Attack Victim." *Yellowstone National Park News Release,* May 24, 2007.

Desch, Heidi. "Night of the grizzlies – 40 years later." *Hungry Horse News,* August 9, 2007.

Grisom, Tom, Publisher. "Condition Upgraded To Fair For Boy Attacked By Bear." *Chattanooga Times Free Press,* April 4, 2006.

Bauman, Joe. "Experts find no odd factors in bear attack." *Deseret News,* June 20, 2007.

Manson, Pamela. "Feds ask for dismissal of suit over bear attack in American Fork Canyon." *The Salt Lake Tribune,* November 19, 2008.

Hartmann, Bruce, President. "8-year-old boy, father injured in Smokies bear attack." *Knoxville News Sentinel,* August 11, 2008.

Hartmann, Bruce, President. "Family recounts attack." *Knoxville New Sentinel,* August 13, 2008.

Christensen, Neils. "Man survives polar bear attack." *Northern News Services,* September 3, 2003.

Neary, Derek, Coordinating Editor. Grolar bear. *Northern News Services,* March 2, 2009.

Smetzer, Mary Beth. "Polar bear killed near village in interior Alaska." *Fairbanks Daily News-Miner,* March 28, 2008.

Kavanagh, LeAnn, Publisher. "The Death of Craig Dahl." *The Glacier Reporter,* June 11, 1998.

Raines, Elaine, for Managing Editor, "Bear mauls girl on Mt. Lemmon." *Arizona Daily Star,* July 26, 1996.

Reports

Alaska State Troopers, Report Status re: Richard and Katherine Huffman, deceased (bear predation), Alaska Department of Public Safety, February 26, 2009.

Alaska State Troopers, Case Information re: Lynn Keough and Buddy Ray Van Dixon, bear mauling. Alaska Department of Public Safety, file closed April 13, 2007.

Alaska State Troopers, Case Information re: Gene Moe, bear mauling. Alaska Department of Public Safety, file closed November 1, 1999.

Alaska State Troopers, Case Information re: Ned Rassmussen, deceased (bear mauling). Alaska Department of Public Safety, file closed December 16, 1999.

Alaska State Troopers, Case Information re: Harley Sievenpiper, deceased (bear predation). Alaska Department of Public Safety, file closed November 9, 1988.

Alaska State Troopers, Case Information re: Timothy Treadwell and Amie Huguenard, deceased (bear predation). Alaska Department of Public Safety, file closed January 8, 2004.

Alaska State Troopers, Case Information re: Marcella Trent and Larry Waldron, deceased (bear mauling). Alaska Department of Public Safety, file closed July 1, 1995.

Alaska State Troopers, Case Information re: Daniel Bigley, bear mauling. Alaska Department of Public Safety, file closed September 5, 2003.

Alaska Wildlife Troopers, Case Information re: Charles Vandergaw, bear feeding. Alaska Department of Public Safety, file closed July 26, 2005.

Smith, Tom. "Bear Pepper Spray: Research and Information." U.S. Geological Survey, 2008.

Youngblood, Gary. Gates of the Arctic National Park Incident Record: Jo Ann Staples (bear mauling). September 24, 2008.

INDEX

9 780984 051595